PRAYING THE NEWS

In 2004, hopeless and desperate people began to pray in Manchester, Kentucky, and the Lord gave us a plan to march through our city. Sixty-three churches and more than 3,500 people marched in a cold rain, and that march gave the Church a voice. The Lord took us from the city of dope to the *city of hope*! Today, we are living in a time when many are discouraged and have given up. The Church in America needs to fall on its knees again and cry out to the only One who can help. This book is a book of *hope*! Allow the Lord to stir you as you read these stories of encouragement. It is a timely book that can change your life.

Doug Abner
Senior Pastor, Community Church, Manchester, Kentucky

I've worked in a lot of newsrooms in my life, but to lead a team of journalists who value and understand the power of prayer is both humbling and thrilling. In *Praying the News*, Wendy and Craig capture the responsibility and excitement that comes from partnering with God to change the headlines.

Rob Allman
News Director, The Christian Broadcasting Network

God said that if we pray, He will hear us and heal our land (see 2 Chron. 7:14). With so many negative reports in the news, Wendy and Craig show us that prayer can take that helpless feeling and turn it into hope that God has a game plan in the midst of pain and chaos. *Praying the News* will inspire you to take your assigned place in God's army as a prayer warrior and stand in that position of prayer patiently as God answers your plea for help, direction and wisdom.

Rebecca Alonzo
Speaker and Author of *The Devil in Pew Number Seven*

Jesus promised that He would send the Holy Spirit and that He would guide us into all truth. We have seen in Toronto, and around the world as this blessing has spread, that we need to make room for the Holy Spirit to lead us. In *Praying the News*, Craig von Buseck and Wendy Griffith show how Spirit-led intercession can change the headlines—and change history.

John and Carol Arnott
Founders, Catch the Fire Ministries

Many years ago, God showed me the vital importance of prayer in the life of every believer—and every ministry. The foundational principle of prayer is that God speaks to our hearts by His Spirit, and then we respond in prayer and move His heart. *Praying the News* demonstrates the biblical truth that the Church is called to be an eternal house of intercession.

Mike Bickle
Director, International House of Prayer, Kansas City, Missouri

It's one thing to be interviewed by a news reporter on TheCall prayer gatherings but it is a wholly different experience to be interviewed by a news reporter who carries the spirit of TheCall within her. Throughout TheCall history, Wendy Griffith and CBN have been there with us, not just reporting but interceding and praying for us. This book by Wendy and Craig von Buseck will put TheCall in your heart because it flows from the sanctuary of Wendy and Craig's experience and life before God. Wendy, you are an Esther on the stage of history for this moment in America. Esther called the nation to prayer, and this book is that call.

Lou Engle
Executive Director of Justice House of Prayer and TheCall

As I have ministered with Craig von Buseck and Wendy Griffith at the Christian Broadcasting Network, I have witnessed firsthand their commitment to a life of prayer. In *Praying the News*, they share stories of how God moved in miraculous ways when they sought Him in intercession and lay a biblical foundation for those who desire to see God move in the same way in their lives. You will be blessed and challenged by this book.

Marguerite Evans
CBN.com Spiritual Gifts Webcast Co-host
Founder, Marguerite Evans Ministries

In *Praying the News,* Craig von Buseck and Wendy Griffith issue a call to believers to arise as watchmen and intercessors to declare God's purposes in the earth. This book will revolutionize your prayer life as you learn to watch and pray from a new and powerful prophetic perspective. It is a must-read for all who want to see God's kingdom come on earth as it is in heaven.

Drs. Tom and Jane Hamon
Senior Leaders, Christian International

For every citizen who is truly concerned about the future of our nation and world, *Praying the News* is one of the most important books you will read. As a Christian who believes that power through prayer is still available to the Church today, I am thrilled that a book like this has been written. Given the condition of our world today, I could not imagine a more timely resource than this. Get ready for a book that will deepen both your intimacy with God and your personal impact for Christ.

Alex McFarland
Bestselling Author, *The 10 Most Common Objections to Christianity*
Co-host, *Explore the Word* Radio Show

For all of us, the "news" is not only part of our daily lives but also is critical to our understanding of the world in which we live. *Praying the News* brings an important perspective: prayer changes things, even the news. Wendy Griffith and Craig von Buseck have penned a must-read book.

Jay Sekulow
Chief Counsel, American Center for Law and Justice

For years I have been interested in praying the Scriptures. Now, Wendy Griffith and Craig von Buseck have given us a way to start praying the news. What better person to teach us how to become intercessors of the events in our world than Wendy, who is a news anchor for the *700 Club*? Let's all start praying the news.

Elmer L. Towns
Co-founder, Liberty University
Dean, School of Religion and Liberty Baptist Theological Seminary
Bestselling Author, *How to Pray When You Don't Know What to Say* and *Fasting for Spiritual Breakthrough*

The world is experiencing an onslaught of terrorism, natural disasters and evil powers. Daily news often brings fear, hopelessness and desperation. Wendy Griffith and Craig von Buseck have written a powerful book that equips intercessors to change these tragedies into times of victory. Practical help is provided so that the person praying is armed and ready for battle. I highly recommend *Praying the News* for anyone desiring to be used by God to help change the world.

Barbara Wentroble
President, International Breakthrough Ministries
President, Breakthrough Business Network
Author, *Prophetic Intercession, Praying with Authority* and *Rise to Your Destiny, Woman of God*

CBN NEWS CO-ANCHOR WENDY GRIFFITH
& CRAIG VON BUSECK CBN.COM

PRAYING
THE NEWS

Your Prayers Are More Powerful than You Know
Discover How You Can Help Those In Need and Change the World

Regal

From Gospel Light
Ventura, California, U.S.A.

Published by Regal
From Gospel Light
Ventura, California, U.S.A.
www.regalbooks.com
Printed in the U.S.A.

Library of Congress Cataloging-in-Publication Data
Griffith, Wendy.
Praying the news / Wendy Griffith, Craig von Buseck.
p. cm.
Includes bibliographical references (p.   ).
ISBN 978-0-8307-5926-2 (trade paper)
1. Prayer—Christianity. 2. Broadcast journalism. 3. Christianity and culture.
I. Von Buseck, Craig. II. Title.
BV210.3.G75 2011
248.3'2—dc23
2011024114

Rights for publishing this book outside the U.S.A. or in non-English languages are
administered by Gospel Light Worldwide, an international not-for-profit ministry.
For additional information, please visit www.glww.org, email info@glww.org, or write
to Gospel Light Worldwide, 1957 Eastman Avenue, Ventura, CA 93003, U.S.A.

To order copies of this book and other Regal products in bulk quantities,
please contact us at 1-800-446-7735.

DEDICATION

To my heavenly Father, who always invites me to pray and partner with Him, and who gives us the desires of our hearts as we delight in Him (see Ps. 37:4). Also to my parents. I love you. Because of you, I have been able to pursue my dreams with no fear, as I always knew that I had a place to call home.

Wendy Griffith

To my wife, Robin. Your passion for Jesus and your heart for intercession inspires me, and many others, to seek God with the same zeal. Your love for our heavenly Father shines through you—and it is marvelous in my eyes.

Craig von Buseck

CONTENTS

FOREWORD

Years ago as I prayed early in the morning in my study, the Lord began showing me principles of Scripture that were as irrefutable as the laws of gravity and thermodynamics. The spiritual laws I discovered in this time of prayer became the guiding principles for The Christian Broadcasting Network (CBN) and the basis for my bestselling book *The Secret Kingdom*.

During another time of prayer, the Lord showed me that He wanted CBN to engage the culture by reporting on current events. This changed the way we presented The 700 Club and gave birth to CBN News.

Jesus demonstrated the essential nature of prayer throughout His earthly ministry, teaching us to pray, "thy Kingdom come, thy will be done." I learned from His example that prayer is the most powerful tool we have to change our lives, our communities and the world.

At CBN, we have made prayer a priority. Every day at noon our employees gather to pray for the needs of the ministry, the needs of our partners, for Israel, and for revival in the world.

On The 700 Club, we don't only report the news; as the Holy Spirit leads, we pray the news as well. As a result, we have seen God do miraculous things—and we have seen the headlines change.

In *Praying the News,* Wendy Griffith of CBN News and Craig von Buseck of CBN.com have challenged believers to engage the culture where they live, becoming a part of God's army of intercessors who are changing the headlines through prayer.

Instead of becoming angry, fearful or cynical when watching or reading the news, Wendy and Craig encourage Christians to allow the news to spur them on to a ministry of intercession. Combining biblical teaching on the need for prayer along with compelling stories of how the headlines changed when God's people prayed, this book is a call to declare "thy Kingdom come, thy will be done" to the world in which we live.

This book shows that when we pray the news in faith, God will hear from heaven, and will heal our land (see 2 Chron. 7:14) More than ever before, we need God's people to rise up in prayer today as His ambassadors in the earth. Now is the time for the Church to truly be God's ministers of reconciliation through prayer and action (see 2 Cor. 5).

When you pray in faith, God will hear your cry, and you will see the headlines change. As Wendy and Craig have shown in this important book, your prayers are more powerful than you know.

Dr. Pat Robertson

PREFACE

The effective prayer of a righteous man can accomplish much.
JAMES 5:16

I (Wendy) almost didn't turn on the television that night. I was on vacation in Myrtle Beach, South Carolina. The sounds of the ocean were so soothing and peaceful, just what the doctor ordered after a busy few weeks in the newsroom. But, for some reason, I turned on the TV and saw CNN's "Breaking News" banner. Wolf Blitzer was saying the President was about to make an important announcement, but he wouldn't or couldn't say what it was. I immediately turned to FOX. *Geraldo at Large* was on, and the FOX News banner was already up: "Osama bin Laden Dead!"

Could it be true? I wondered. *Could the world's most feared, most hated and perhaps most diabolical terrorist really be dead?*

With a gleam in his eye, President Obama confirmed to the world that the terror mastermind of 9-11 was indeed dead. "And on nights like this one," he said, "we can say to those families who have lost loved ones to al-Qaeda's terror: Justice has been done." The President also praised the more than two-dozen brave Navy Seals who risked their lives to raid the terrorist's compound in Pakistan and take down the al-Qaeda leader.

But why did it take so long? Many have wondered why the man who inflicted so much pain on a nation and who sent nearly 3,000 people on 9-11 to an untimely death could have stayed "on the loose" for nearly a decade. But, as Christians, we know that the issues of justice and mercy are in the hands of the Lord. In Romans 12:19, Paul says, "Do not take revenge, my friends, but leave room for God's wrath, for it is written: 'It is mine to avenge: I will repay, says the Lord' " (*NIV*).

Yes, it is our job as people of faith to pray for peace, and it is our job to intercede for justice that evil may be thwarted. But it is always in the hand of God to bring that justice in His wisdom and time. As Proverbs 24:17 states, "Do not gloat [celebrate] when your enemy falls; when he stumbles, do not let your heart rejoice" (*NIV*).

When I (Craig) heard the news of bin Laden's death, I also thought about the issues of mercy and justice as I considered the great irony of the moment. On that fateful day in May 2011, I was attending the Global Christian Internet Alliance conference in California when I heard of bin Laden's death. Amazingly, on September 11, 2001, I had been in an airplane heading to another Internet evangelism conference when the attacks occurred.

I thought of the power of words and motives. Here was a man who used his speech to bring fear, death and destruction to people around the world. As I looked around the room at this group of Internet evangelists, I prayed that each of them would use the Internet to communicate the gospel of peace and love in Jesus Christ to counter the words of fear and hate that had been espoused by Osama bin Laden.

Prayer Changes the Course of History

When people pray in sincerity and unity according to the will of God revealed in the Bible, things change; headlines change. The ancient words of the apostle James are just as true today as they were when he wrote them under the inspiration of the Holy Spirit in the first century AD: "The effective prayer of a righteous man can accomplish much" (Jas. 5:16).

We have seen the truth of this scriptural admonition powerfully demonstrated in recent events that have affected every person living on planet Earth. In a moment, not so long ago, life as we knew it changed forever. On that day, as a deep blue heaven extended over the horizon like a cloudless canopy, a fiery arrow suddenly raced across this peaceful sky in the form of a hijacked airplane.

That day was September 11, 2001.

The events of this day reminded us that there is still a spiritual enemy who comes like a thief to "steal and kill and destroy." But we also know that Christ is alive in the earth today and that He came "that they may have life, and have it abundantly" (John 10:10).

We know from Scripture that Christ is building His Church in the world today, but in these uncertain times that Church sometimes seems unaware—or even ambivalent—to the fact that Jesus desires to use His people as a spiritual force in the earth to work with Him to destroy the works of darkness. In Matthew 16:19, He declares of the Church that "all the powers of hell will not conquer it" (Matt. 16:18, *NLT*).

One of the primary ways that God is using the Church to defeat the powers of hell is through prayer (see Eph. 6:10-12,19). The need for committed believers to rise up in this ministry of intercession was never more clearly demonstrated than after the attacks of September 11, 2001. Beginning that fateful day, believers around the world began praying the news. They prayed that the families of the victims would be comforted and healed. They also prayed that those who committed those terrible crimes would renounce their evil ways and, like Saul of Tarsus on the road to Damascus, they would commit themselves to the gospel of peace through Jesus Christ.

Wendy's 9-11 Prayer

That morning, I (Wendy) was working behind the scenes at the Christian Broadcasting Network (CBN), gathering news for *The 700 Club*. It was a beautiful September morning, and everything was going smoothly. Suddenly, as I sat in one of our production suites, my editor and I watched in amazement as the TV monitor showed a plane slamming into one of the World Trade Center towers. Then, minutes later, we watched a plane fly into the other tower.

At first I thought they were replaying the first plane slamming into the building. Then I realized it was a live feed. They had struck again. It was surreal, and too terrible to comprehend.

Immediately, *The 700 Club* went live on the air and CBN News went into high gear. I was running information out to Pat Robertson in the studio as fast as I could. Pat immediately called the Church to prayer, leading in intercession from our headquarters in Virginia Beach. Over the next several hours he remained calm as he gave viewers a play-by-play of the terrible tragedy that had just taken place in our nation.

Later that day, the CBN News team gathered for a meeting to pray and receive our assignments. Within days, my crew and I arrived in New York City as clouds of dark smoke still billowed from the rubble. It was an eerie sight. Fear gripped the city, and I could sense it clearly in my spirit. As I worked to gather the story, I too had the feeling that another plane could fall from the sky at any moment. Perhaps the jihadists would continue their terror campaign by blowing up buildings.

All I knew was that life would never be the same.

As I checked into my Times Square hotel, the uneasy feeling persisted. *What if the terrorists aren't done? What if they're just getting warmed up?* I cried out in prayer for God's peace, but it was slow in coming.

Then, as I entered my room on the twelfth floor of the Algonquin Hotel, something I saw gave me peace. Hanging on the wall over the bed was a simple painting of a country church set amidst rolling hills, with a group of people walking together through the doorway. Perhaps it's because I'm from West Virginia, but God knew that painting would comfort me. I knew it was God saying, "I'm with you. You're going to be all right. You're right where I want you to be."

And then things got even better. My sister, JeanAnne, who was a flight attendant for U.S. Airways at the time, called and told me she was grounded in New York for several days and was staying at a hotel only one block away! My sister was able to go with me on several interviews, and we were able to have dinner together in a city that was still in a state of shock.

The Lord gave me His peace and comfort in the middle of the worst terror attack in the history of our nation. God was still in charge—even if all hell seemed to be breaking lose.

Craig's 9-11 Airplane Ride

It was just after 6:00 A.M. on the morning of September 11, 2001, as I (Craig) boarded the plane at Williamsburg Airport and settled into my seat. The first sliver of turquoise-colored sky began to inch upward from above the tree line at the edge of the runway. I looked up the aisle just in time to see a young man of Middle Eastern descent. He wore a long robe and a turban on his head. A friend of mine was killed when the Marine Corps barracks in Beirut, Lebanon, was bombed in 1983. Since that time, I had been very aware of the threat of terrorism. When this man walked down the aisle of that aircraft, my first thought was, "Could this person be a terrorist?"

I transferred from one plane to another in Atlanta, and soon we departed for Chicago. I had seen videotape of Osama bin Laden and his terrorist training camps in Afghanistan, and I remembered the chilling scenes of the terrorists breaking into rooms and shooting mannequins with crosses or Star of David symbols painted on them. As I looked out the window over the patchwork of farms, I had no inkling of the horror that my fellow countrymen were facing from these terrorists at that very moment. During my two-hour flight, American Airlines Flight 11 hit the north tower of the World Trade Center at 8:45 A.M.; then United Airlines Flight 175 slammed into the south tower, going 500 miles an hour, at 9:03 A.M. Then American Airlines Flight 77 crashed into the Pentagon at 9:40 A.M. as we began our descent into Chicago.

The passengers on my flight were unaware that our nation had plunged into chaos as we flew across America's heartland. We landed at Midway Airport in Chicago, and as I looked out of my window, I noticed a police car racing down an adjacent runway with its blue lights flashing. As we taxied toward the terminal, I noticed another police cruiser, also with its lights flashing, sitting in front of a gate next to the road. *What is going on?* I wondered.

Our plane suddenly screeched to a halt out in the middle of the airfield. Within moments the pilot spoke over the intercom. "We will need to stay here on the tarmac for a moment as we wait for the airport to open a gate for us." I wondered if this strange announcement had anything to do with the police cars. A moment later, the captain gave the passengers permission to use their cell phones. Suddenly, a voice from behind me spoke in a loud tone, "Terrorists have hit the World Trade Center with an airplane."

Throughout the fuselage passengers were turning on their cell phones and receiving the news that was now being broadcast around the world. Instantly, the aircraft was abuzz with conversation. "They also hit the second tower," someone cried out. "The Pentagon has been attacked," another voice cried out.

Radical Muslim terrorists. The thought was immediate. My mind flashed back to major terrorist attacks in recent years: the bomb in the parking garage of the World Trade Center; the murderous attack on the *U.S.S. Cole*; the embassy bombings in Kenya and Tanzania; the explosion at the Khobar Towers in Dhahran, Saudi Arabia . . .

After a few minutes, the airplane eased forward and we pulled into a hastily cleared gate. A security agent armed with a machine gun met us at the door. He was allowing passengers off the plane and keeping others from getting on. I hurried to the nearest television set where a large number of people had gathered to witness for the first time the images of the burning World Trade Center towers. Within minutes I watched video of the tragic collapse of these magnificent structures.

I couldn't believe what I was seeing and hearing. Shaking my head, I lifted up a silent prayer for the people in harm's way, for the families of the victims, for the rescuers, for the President and for America. As I watched those horrible images, I declared aloud, "Our lives have just changed forever. It will never be the same."

Spirit-led Prayer Begins

The world indeed changed forever on September 11, 2001, and yet, in many ways, it remains much the same. We have discovered yet again in our modern age that the words of Solomon remain true: "There is nothing new under the sun" (Eccles. 1:9).

In those days after September 11, Wendy and I, and many others, carried out our ministry duties for CBN in an ongoing attitude of prayer—joining the intercession of countless other believers across America and around the world. Even before the attacks, though, the Spirit of God was leading certain people in intercession—and that made all the difference to the outcome on September 11.

September 10 was the anniversary of the day that Delores and Ken Liesner met. But their usual plans to celebrate were overshadowed by an ominous feeling of danger that Delores tried to keep to herself. "First I suggested we cancel our original plans and stay home on the tenth. But Ken was determined to celebrate in some small way, so on September 9, we headed toward a Frank Lloyd-Wright home about 90 miles to the west."

Reading from the book *Names of the Holy Spirit*, they were discussing Nehemiah 9:20: "You gave Your good Spirit to instruct them." But as they drove, the unsettling aura increased in Delores's spirit.

"It's hard to hide anything when you've been with someone for 40 years," Delores remembers. "I strained to hear or see what I thought I could 'feel' was approaching as we drove along. I knew my unrest had not gone unnoticed when Ken softly asked, 'What is it? What's bothering you?' His question forced me to crack a small, tight smile. 'I don't know yet,' was my honest answer as I nervously glanced out my side window again.

"Ken questioned if we should turn back, and I hesitantly confessed to an eerie feeling that something ominous—something dark and evil—was going to happen soon. I didn't know what I was feeling or watching for, but I felt it coming from an area I pointed to outside the passenger window. When we got home, Ken pinpointed the area as the northeastern United States.

"We could not pull over, as the rain was forceful, and so we began to pray through our concerns, listing the family and loved ones as they came to mind. When we mentioned our niece Trinity and her husband, Larry, I became overwhelmed with concern for them. They live far from us in New York, and we don't see them very often. We continued to pray for them off and on during our trip that day, over lunch and then again on the return home.

"I thought of calling Trinity, but I feared my 'dark' worries might seem silly to her. So I decided to leave it with the Lord. The next day, my concern grew hourly, and I did not sleep that night—September 10. I spent the day praying over the list of our family and ministries, but frequently came back to Trinity and Larry. I wondered what physical or spiritual need Trinity and Larry could be facing to have such an unusually compelling control over my heart and mind. I determined to make a call the next day to see if there was anything I could do.

"It was difficult for me to keep my mind on work the next morning because of the lack of sleep and the early hour that I go to the office. Frequent glances at the clock showed me it was too early to call. Each time I checked the time I prayed for them again, mystified at the continued feeling of oppression, darkness and concern for my niece's family.

"At 9:15 A.M., I was called to the outer office where staff had gathered around a TV monitor to watch news of the attack on the World Trade Center. Instantly, I understood the previous 48 hours of turmoil. Larry worked near the World Trade Center and frequently stopped at a coffee shop there on his way to work. I ran to my office and called my sister. Without even a hello, she answered, 'Larry and Trinity are okay. He had not left for work yet.' "

Then Delores's sister shared the rest of the story with her. Trinity and Larry had planned a little family outing at the mall beneath the World Trade Center prior to Larry's scheduled work time. They were going to take the subway there, eat breakfast and shop before he went to work. The evening before, the couple's usually happy baby had several brief periods of fussiness, with no obvious illness or reason. They were finally able to rest in the early morning hours and consequently overslept. Awakened by a call from Larry's mother, they rushed to the television and saw the horrific scene. Their eyes met with one thought: *We would have been there.*

"My sister was astounded when I shared with her about the prayer vigil Ken and I had held for them."

Delores explains that the Bible calls us to this kind of Spirit-led prayer in Luke 21:36: "Keep on the alert at all times, praying that you may have strength to escape all these things that are about to take place, and to stand before the Son of Man." "If you do this," she adds, "God's good Spirit will guide you."[1]

Praying the News After 9-11

In the days following the 9-11 attacks, Anne Arvizu was obsessed with the news. "I couldn't get enough, and I couldn't stop crying as

I prayed for victims to be recovered from the pile of ash and smoke. I wanted so badly to go and help, but they didn't really need any pharmacists, so I resigned myself to the understanding that all I could do was pray."

A few weeks after the event, "the phenomenon," as Anne called it, started to manifest. Once or twice a day, for months, it was as if an invisible hand would guide Anne's chin and point her head toward the clock each day at one time and one time only. Whether it was morning or night, her attention would be interrupted, seemingly supernaturally, and refocused to a digital clock blinking 9:11.

"At first, as this 'phenomenon' unfolded in my life, I'd see the number and start to cry. After it happened for weeks on end, I remember having a conversation with the Lord, and saying to Him, 'This can't be a coincidence, God.'

"I was always distracted, absorbed in conversation, looking somewhere completely different, and then I would turn my head and notice the numbers 9:11. Or the sound of the dryer buzzing would startle me and I'd look up at exactly 9:11. Or a phone call would come in and jolt me to walk to the phone near the oven at 9:11.

"No matter how many different ways it happened, I'd find myself thinking, *God? Is this You? This is more than me just noticing this time. I am not intentionally or subconsciously drawing my attention to it; it just happens. What should I do with this?*"

The answer that came to Anne was crystal clear. She says, "There were no thundering voices, no real responses from God, but I felt the undeniable clear direction to pray for exactly one minute every time I saw it."

In the early months, it was quite a challenge. She would pray and then open one eye when she was finished only to find that it was not yet 9:12. At that time, one minute of directed, intercessory prayer was a long time! "I could finish up all the obvious prayers I prayed on 9/11/01 collectively and still seem to have time left over for repeats."

For months, Anne continued to pray for the victims and their families, for the nation and its leaders and for the soul of the country. As time went by, and as she remained faithful to this calling of intercession, her prayers began to grow longer and deeper. Surface prayers became soul questions: *How do I pray for my enemies?*

"I'd pray for the attackers—Abraham's seed, a nation that God had blessed at Abraham's request through Ishmael. I'd weep for a lost nation that God loves and its radical factions that demonstrate hate. I'd seek Scripture on prayer and then pray through them, thanking God for His grace in my life, since I once was lost. I'd pray through the Lord's Prayer aloud, asking for His kingdom to come and His will to be done.

"When I'd run out of things to pray, I'd intercede in my heavenly prayer language—an all-but-unused gift in the church in which I was planted. But in my prayer closet I'd use my gift of tongues to let the Holy Spirit groan His way through me. I didn't need an eschatological, theoretical, hermeneutical or even theological reason for doing what I was doing. I just longed to be used by God to pray in any way I could, for as long as needed."

Sometimes Anne would pray until she felt the release of joy in her spirit. Other times in prayer she would be deeply moved for specific victims of terror and oppression around the world—brothels in India, little boys traded and sodomized as prostitutes for men in Nicaragua, oppressed and mutilated women in East Africa . . .

"I'd weep for them as Jesus wept for Jerusalem. It seemed that the more I'd watch the news, the more deeply disturbed I felt in my spirit and the more I had to pray. It was as if I could feel the Holy Spirit grieve over the state of the world."

Now, after years of intercessory prayer, Anne has developed somewhat of a routine to help her stay focused. Choice websites and documentaries give her headline news, and her husband provides any other relevant details she needs, to know how to pray. As a result of yielding to the Spirit's leading to pray the news after the September 11 attacks, Anne's prayer and devotional life have been revolutionized.

She says, "During those first few weeks, I could never have imagined that a decade later I'd look back and still be prompted in similar ways to pray for all those affected by 9-11. I also never could have predicted the way my prayer life would expand so deeply—

from struggling to get through an entire minute to spending hours or days dedicated to prayer, and now living a daily life in constant communion and conversation with God.

"I may never know this side of heaven the impact of my little one-minute prayers; but as the Bible says, obedience is better than sacrifice. What I do know is that God used this urge to pray after 9-11 as 'the call before the call.' Before I could truly follow the path He was going to lay before me, I had to bear up and strengthen the most important call we have as Christians: the call to pray."

Anne explains that the call to pray returns each of us to our walk with God in the cool of the Garden. Through Christ, this prayer life leads us to the state of living out our most important relationship: intimacy with our Father.[2]

Prayer in the Aftermath of 9-11

In the days following the September 11 terrorist attacks, the people of America prayed collectively like they had not prayed in years. Just days later, on September 14, President George W. Bush called for a National Day of Prayer and Remembrance. In his address from the National Cathedral in Washington, DC, President Bush comforted the nation: "We learn in tragedy that His purposes are not always our own, yet the prayers of private suffering, whether in our homes or in this great cathedral, are known and heard and understood."

Among the speakers that day was the Rev. Billy Graham. He stood before the nation and declared, "Today we especially come together in this service to confess our need of God. We've always needed God, from the very beginning of this nation, but today we need Him especially. We're facing a new kind of enemy. We're involved in a new kind of warfare, and we need the help of the Spirit of God. The Bible's words are our hope: 'God is our refuge and strength, an ever-present help in trouble. Therefore we will not fear'" (Ps. 46:1-2, *NIV*).

Though churches were filled to capacity in those first days after 9-11, it wasn't long before the people turned back to their normal routines and church was forgotten. The prayers that were so fervent soon cooled, and in many cases, ceased altogether. But the danger in our world remains. The threat of terrorism is just as real today as it was in 2001. And we face many other serious threats as well. Never before has faith-filled prayer by God's people been more needed. Like Anne Arvizu, God is calling people of faith to rise up in this tumultuous time and pray for His will to be done and His kingdom to come on earth as it is in heaven.

This book is an invitation to you to be a part of this army of prayer warriors that God is raising up to declare and agree with His purposes in the earth. Today, He gives you this charge and promise:

> Be wise in what is good and innocent in what is evil. The God of peace will soon crush Satan under your feet (Rom. 16:19-20).

Today God is calling every disciple of Jesus Christ into this same place of agreeing with Him in prayer to see His loving purposes established in the earth. Instead of becoming angry or frustrated while watching or reading the news, will you allow God to do the same redemptive work in you that He did in Anne? Today He is asking you to yield to His Spirit and heed the call to "Pray the News." Will you answer the call?

1

WE'VE GOT TO
PRAY JUST TO MAKE
IT TODAY

Singer MC Hammer may have been the first to sing the words, "We've got to pray just to make it today," but the reality is, without prayer, nothing of importance is accomplished. Back in the eighteenth century, theologian John Wesley famously said, "God does nothing except in response to believing prayer."

Dr. Vinson Synan of Regent University found these words to be more true than he could ever have imagined. In the late 1980s, Dr. Synan was attending a Charismatic leadership conference when a Mennonite bishop stood and declared, "We need to pray about the nuclear arms race." In those days, it seemed as if Communism, through its various tentacles, would engulf the world. Across the globe, from Vietnam to Angola, countries were falling to Communist tyranny. At the time, Synan didn't think much about those kinds of things but was more concerned with the moving of the Holy Spirit. But this bishop's comment touched his heart, leading him to believe that this was something he ought to pray about more seriously. Over time, this prayer need began to dominate his thinking.

In early 1989, Synan was attending a meeting of the board for the California Theological Seminary, so he was staying in a hotel near Pebble Beach Golf Course. Having a day off, he decided to play a round of golf at this famous landmark. Driving along the Pacific Coast Highway, he took in the beautiful scenery. But as he made his way along the coastline, the only thing that kept running through his mind was the nuclear arms race. "How do I pray?" he finally cried out to God.

Suddenly a question came into his mind: *What would be the best possible thing that could happen, short of war and bloodshed, to stop this arms race?*

"It came to me suddenly," Synan remembers. "The best thing would be if Communism collapsed from the inside without a war. And the Lord said, 'Why don't you pray for that?'"

Immediately, he pulled over to the side of the road, stopped the car and shut the motor off. He lifted his hands and for 20 minutes fervently prayed that Communism would collapse, shifting from prayer in English to prayer in his heavenly tongue.

"My mind kept objecting, because Communism seemed so permanent. They were supposed to take over the world. My whole adult life had been under the shadow of the Cold War, the atomic bomb and the threat of inevitable Communist expansion. In Europe it seemed utterly permanent. But the Lord said, 'Pray that it will collapse.' I thought that this was impossible, but I did what God asked me to do."

"I prayed fervently in the Spirit. I had never prayed quite like that before. Then, after 20 minutes, the burden lifted and I went on to the golf course."

Later that year, Dr. Synan spoke to a group of Pentecostal ministers at the Lake Yale campground in Florida and prophesied that the Berlin Wall would fall. "I didn't make a big deal about it, but I remembered that John Wesley said, 'God does nothing, but by prayer.'"

On November 10, 1989, Dr. Synan was presiding over another Charismatic conference in Indianapolis, Indiana. He was staying in the home of a local minister named Larry Miles. That morning, before he could even get out of bed, he was awakened by Larry calling out, "Vinson, get up. You won't believe what's on television." He rushed to the set and watched as the German people stood triumphantly on top of the Berlin wall, chipping at it with pick axes and hammers, tearing it down before his eyes.

"I watched thousands of people chipping away and finally bringing down the first piece of the wall, and I remembered that time of intercessory prayer on the way to the golf course."

During that same season, Dr. Ted Baehr of *Movieguide* was also praying for the fall of godless Communism. When the head of the KGB secret police, Yuri Andropov, became Secretary General of the

Communist Party in the Soviet Union, he made some strong, disparaging anti-Christian remarks. This attack elicited intense prayer from Christians around the world, including Ted.

Baehr felt led by the Holy Spirit to send the Soviet leader a letter calling him to account for his sins. "The letter told him to repent and be saved, and explained to him the eternal consequences of his actions," Baehr said.

One week after Andropov's staff acknowledged that the premier had received and read the letter, on February 9, 1984, the Soviet leader died suddenly and passed on to judgment.

"It is clear that many people around the world would have been concerned enough about his comments to pray," Baehr reflects, "and it is also clear that God reigns in the lives of men. Sooner or later, everyone is called to account."[1]

"I think the Lord was looking for intercessors to pray the impossible," said Synan. "It just so happened that burden fell on me. I'm not claiming any credit whatsoever. It was just a burden about world events; that things would change. I pray now about the Islamic jihadist terrorists. We need more Christians now to intercede for that murderous group of extremists to collapse, without war. But God can do things that man cannot even comprehend."

Changing History Through Praying the News

We live at a time in history when it is critical for the Church to learn to be led by the Spirit like this in prayer. God wants to raise up a company of intercessors to pray the news—which is to watch, read or listen to the news, then intercede for God's will to be done in the issues we face today.

God desires that His people become so in tune with His Spirit—as Vinson Synan and Ted Baehr were regarding the Communist threat—that we are actually praying His will in advance of world events. By cooperating with God in prayer, we are actually helping to shape those events in the spirit realm.

God is seeking prayer warriors who will agree with Him in faith to actually make an impact on the course of history through their intercession, by walking in the Spirit. The apostle Paul wrote of the privilege and importance of the believer to live in the Spirit: "For all who are being led by the Spirit of God, these are sons of God" (Rom. 8:14).

Far too often, we, the Church, have been reactionary in our prayers—a tragedy or a disaster happens, and believers react with "catch-up prayers." But we serve the God who sees the end from the beginning. He desires that we be so in-tune with His Spirit that we are praying His perfect will in a circumstance before it ever occurs in the natural.

This sensitivity to the leading of the Holy Spirit only comes by maintaining a daily intimate relationship with our Father and our Lord Jesus Christ. Jesus revealed this concept when He told His disciples:

> Abide in Me, and I in you. As the branch cannot bear fruit of itself unless it abides in the vine, so neither can you unless you abide in Me. I am the vine, you are the branches; he who abides in Me and I in him, he bears much fruit, for apart from Me you can do nothing (John 15:4-5).

As we put the first commandment first—to love the Lord our God with all our heart, soul, mind and strength—He then empowers us by His Spirit to fulfill the second commandment—to love our neighbor (and our city, our nation and this world) by being led by the Spirit in intercession.

Judson Cornwall writes of the importance of Spirit-led intercession that flows from us as a result of abiding in God:

> There are times when we desperately need to know more than what God is doing and saying. We need to know God, for He works according to His nature and will, and only an understanding of that nature and will enables us to be involved with Him before His actions are demonstrated. We do not need to have great knowledge of God to know what God is saying if He is saying it publicly; but if God chooses to withhold communicated knowledge and yet we know the

heart of God, there will be an intuitive or spiritual understanding that gives us knowledge out of relationship with God, not too unlike the understanding that develops between a husband and wife who have lived in a loving relationship for many years.

God does not always forewarn His people of specific actions, but He always invites us into His presence during times of judgment, and in that presence there often comes a spiritual knowing of the ways of the Lord. Too often the modern Church seems to be playing "catch-up" in Her ministry of intercession because Her relationship with God is out of date. This forces the Church to deal with God about what He has done, not what He is doing, much less be able to intercede with Him about what He is going to do.

David wrote, "He made known His ways to Moses, His acts to the children of Israel" (Ps. 103:7). A distinguishing difference between Moses and the children of Israel is that Moses knew God's ways, which enabled him to know what God was going to do before He did it; but the congregation knew only God's acts. Obviously, if we know only God's acts, we will know only where God has been and what He has done. If we know only the acts of God, we will forever live in the past. It's time for the Church to know more than what God did. We need to know Who God is! We need to emulate Paul, who cried, "That I may know Him . . ." (Phil. 3:10).[2]

God is seeking this kind of heart in His people today—a heart that cries, "I want to know You, God. And I want to serve You, my Lord." By walking in this type of love relationship with God, we position ourselves to be used by God on the earth. This is especially true in the realm of intercessory prayer.

Shaping History Through Prayer
A key leader in the Church today who has caught this vision to intercede in advance of crisis is Lou Engle. Through TheCall and

other intercessory prayer outreaches, Engle has made a tremendous impact in the spirit realm in recent years. After reading the groundbreaking book *Shaping History Through Prayer and Fasting*, by Derek Prince, Engle's view of prayer changed dramatically:

> I began to fast (with others in our church) and saw an immediate impact in terms of people being saved and set free. Then God opened the door to the city of Pasadena. We ended up having a three-year outpouring of the Holy Spirit several years later here—that I believe was directly related to fasting—where tens of thousands of people came through our doors and were touched mightily by the power of God. In 1994, through an encounter with a group of Taiwanese kids, again the Spirit fell and a sovereign youth movement of prayer started around the nation. We began to hold small, intense prayer gatherings across the nation.[3]

Then in 1996, Lou had a dream in which the Lord directed him to deliver the message of the book of Joel to the nation:

> Call the youth of America to fasting and prayer. We continued to hold gatherings in 1997, 1998, and 1999 that grew to as many as 4,500 kids gathering for three to five days of fasting and prayer. Ultimately, TheCall sprang out of a prophetic vision we received from Promise Keepers: the hearts of the fathers turning to the children. We began to proclaim that the kids were going to go to Washington, D.C., to fast and pray as a counterpart to the Promise Keepers rally, and that it would be a sign that the nation was turning to God. We live in a culture that is so resistant to God and His Spirit that I believe today's generation needs the weapons of fasting and prayer simply to survive.[4]

Praying the News takes up this banner of prayer and fasting and waves it for all generations of Christians. It is time to yield to the

Spirit, as Lou did with TheCall, and declare, "Here we are, God. Use us to pray. Here we are, God. Use us to act."

The White House Intercession Assignment

In the fall of 1997, as I (Craig) was working on my Master's Degree at Regent University, I had a friend who was an assistant to the Dean of the Government School. One night he called to tell me that his car battery had died as he was on the way to a very important Government School advisory board gathering in Washington, DC. The problem was that he had all of the documents and decorations for the meeting in his car. It was imperative that he got to this meeting. My friend asked me to purchase a new battery and meet him on the highway.

In my heart, I felt like I heard the Spirit of God telling me to pack an overnight bag just in case. Sure enough, the new battery didn't work, so we loaded everything into my car and drove to our nation's capital. Arriving at 3 A.M., we checked into the Hay-Adams Hotel, directly across Lafayette Park from the White House.

The next morning my friend woke early to go to his meeting and I was left alone in the hotel room. As I read my Bible and prayed, I inquired of the Lord, "What would You have me do today?" Immediately He spoke to my heart, "Go and walk around the entire circumference of the White House, praying in the Spirit and declaring, 'Let those things that are being done in secret be shouted from the housetops' (Luke 12:3)."

I put on my coat and walked across Lafayette Park to the White House. I slowly approached the perimeter, placing my hand on the iron gate and praying under my breath, "God, You said to intercede for our leaders, so I pray that You would bless President Clinton with wisdom and protection. But, Lord, You have also asked me to make this declaration, so I pray that those things that are being done in secret would be shouted from the housetops."

I turned to my right and began to slowly walk around the large White House complex, stopping from time to time to make the declaration the Lord commanded me—all the while wondering what the Secret Service guards on the roof of the White House were thinking about my prayer journey.

I finally made my way around the entire grounds, finishing my assignment and returning to my hotel. Later that day my friend and I drove back to Virginia Beach.

Several months later, the nation was rocked into a constitutional crisis by the Monica Lewinsky scandal. Like most people, I was shocked at the revelations that were being released in the news media in embarrassing detail. I know that I was only one of tens of thousands of believers who were praying for righteousness in America. But it was with a sad heart that I remembered my intercessory assignment at the White House that cold day only months before.

A Dark Hour: The Impeachment Trial Assignment

Not long after Craig felt called to prayer-walk around the White House, I (Wendy) was given a front row seat to one of the biggest stories of the last century—the impeachment trial of former President William Jefferson Clinton. It was my first assignment with CBN and I could hardly believe my fortune, or perhaps, misfortune. There was a gloom hanging over Washington, DC, that had nothing to do with the cold and dreary winter weather. Our nation was in mourning.

Clinton, who had been impeached by the House of Representatives on December 19, 1998, was facing charges of perjury and obstruction of justice stemming from his effort to cover up a sexual relationship with Monica Lewinsky, a former White House intern. As I sat in the U.S. Senate balcony with other national journalists, I couldn't help but wonder, *What am I doing here? How did a small town girl from West Virginia end up among some of the most famous faces on television, covering one of the most important stories of our time?* I knew it wasn't my journalistic credentials alone that had landed me on Capitol Hill. In my heart I understood that God had put me here, during one of American's darkest hours for a divine purpose.

And that purpose was simply to pray.

My heart ached for our leaders who faced a seemingly impossible decision: to impeach a sitting president and further divide the country, or ignore the fact that he had lied under oath and disgraced our nation with his infidelity.

Star-struck

I had an office the size of a very small closet in the media section of the Senate Chambers. CNN Correspondent Candy Crowley was right across the aisle from me, but I was so star-struck, I never even introduced myself—something I still regret to this day. I was still astounded that I was in the same "league" with these national media stars. I would retreat in there daily to write my stories and often found myself in tears—not only because I felt completely overwhelmed, but because the spiritual warfare for the soul of our nation was so intense.

Looking back, I know I was interceding for our nation, and for some reason my presence was needed. God has His people everywhere. But, believe me, I was out-numbered. There seemed to be few Christians on Capitol Hill at that time. Some other reporters would mock me and say, "What's God saying about this?" As the nation waited for a verdict, I sat with a bird's-eye view of the Senate Chambers, praying that God would give our leaders the wisdom of Solomon. In Proverbs 29:2, Solomon said, "When the righteous are in authority, the people rejoice; but when a wicked man rules, the people groan" (*NKJV*).

The Verdict

On February 12, 1999, the Senate had its say. In a mostly partisan vote, with no Democrats voting to impeach, President Clinton was acquitted of all charges. It was only the second impeachment trial of a president in American history. It turns out that this was just the beginning of the many times I would find myself on the front lines of a national or international crisis where the real assignment—or the most important assignment—was prayer.

Hope for Modern Man?

Prior to World War I there was a group of intellectuals in England called the Fabian Socialists. Their leader was a self-appointed prophet of a new world order, the author H. G. Wells. Members of this group were rationalists and humanists. In 1914, two years before the outbreak of World War I, Wells declared triumphantly, "It is possible for us to have a new race of people by intellectual and biological processes. We don't need the Bible, we don't need the church, we can pull down the hills of wealth, we can fill up the valleys of poverty."

But then the earth was plunged into two horrific World Wars and H. G. Wells lost his rosy optimism. His final book, *Mind at the End of Its Tether*, reflected this new outlook. "There is no hope for humanity. . . . There is a little cavity somewhere in the human breast which can be filled by God and only God."[5]

Apart from God, mankind is lost with no hope. Life for the ungodly quickly descends to merely the pursuit of pleasure. "Eat, drink and be merry, for tomorrow we die," declares cynical modern man. Without God in our lives, this cynicism would be understandable. In this second decade of the new Millennium, we face daunting challenges:

- Terrorism and violence continue to spread.
- After the fall of Communism, radical Islam has risen as the next philosophy bent on world domination.
- We face the worst financial crisis since the Great Depression.
- Not only is there a threat of nuclear war, but now there is a growing threat of an atomic bomb in the hands of a rogue nation.
- Terrorist groups like al-Qaeda are trying to obtain a nuclear device, or "dirty bomb," to spread radiation poisoning in our mega cities.
- There is an epidemic of divorce and broken families.
- More than ever, children are being raised in homes where only one parent is present.
- More than 54 million babies have been aborted in the U.S. alone since the *Roe v. Wade* Supreme Court decision in 1973.[6]
- Drug and alcohol abuse is rampant around the world.
- Violent crime associated with the illegal drug trade has cost the lives of hundreds of thousands.

- Sexually explicit media, pornography, violent movies and video games are among America's most lucrative exports. The United States has earned the moniker "The Great Satan" among Islamists, in part because of the hedonistic media we send around the world.
- Western society has sanctioned open sexual immorality. Traditional biblical values are looked on as naïve, silly, or even oppressive.
- In the media, academia, and even in some churches, the Word of God is mocked, ridiculed, twisted, or ignored completely.

Mankind has, in many ways, turned its back on God. As a society, we have reaped what we have sown through increased violence and crime; an AIDS epidemic and rampant sexually transmitted diseases; public schools that far too often erupt in violence; countless broken homes and unwed pregnancies; and corruption in business and government that has led us to the brink of worldwide financial collapse.

By turning our backs on God, we have made a terrible mess of things. Apart from His intervention, there is little hope. But God has not turned His back on us. He wants to reign in the earth as the Prince of Peace. In Him there is hope for tomorrow. He declares:

> For I know the plans that I have for you . . . plans for welfare and not for calamity to give you a future and a hope (Jer. 29:11).

And He desires to use faithful believers like you to partner with Him in prayer to see His purposes established in the earth. God declares:

> If my people, who are called by my name, will humble themselves and pray and seek my face and turn from their wicked ways, then will I hear from heaven and will forgive their sin and will heal their land (2 Chron. 7:14, NIV).

In His love and compassion, God wants to bring solutions to the problems that plague us. He promises, "When the enemy comes in like a flood, the Spirit of the LORD will lift up a standard against him" (Isa. 59:19, *NKJV*).

Faith-filled believers in the Church today are a significant part of the standard that the Spirit of the Lord is lifting up in the earth. He is calling on Bible-believing Christians to partner with Him in humility and prayer to see "His kingdom come and His will be done, on earth as it is in heaven."

Touching Heaven, Changing Earth

When we see these potentially frightening and devastating things in the news, it can be easy to give in to fear, anger or despair. There is a lot of bad news that is reported on an ongoing basis through 24-hour news channels, and now through our smart phones or iPads. It is easy to become overwhelmed by it all—especially because it is hard to know whom to trust anymore. Mark Twain once said, "A lie can travel half way around the world while the truth is just putting on its shoes." There have been so many news organizations caught in lies that the public has grown cynical, especially of the mainstream media.

There has also been a perception of an anti-Christian, anti-biblical bias in the field of journalism in the last century. Sadly, there are many examples of media hostility toward Christianity and the Bible in America and Western Europe.

But despite those who would fight against biblical truth, Jesus still loves the people of this world. He wants His people to love and pray for the lost. He doesn't want us to fall into anger, cynicism or hopelessness when watching or reading the news. Instead, He calls His disciples to engage the culture through prayer and action: "Do not be overcome by evil, but overcome evil with good" (Rom. 12:21).

God desires for Christians in the world to take up the ministry of Jeremiah, of whom God said:

> Behold, I have put My words in your mouth. See, I have appointed you this day over the nations and over the king-

doms, to pluck up and to break down, to destroy and to overthrow, to build and to plant (Jer. 1:9-10).

Derek Prince explains that like Jeremiah, Christians stand in a twofold relationship to the secular government: "On the natural plane, as a citizen of Judah, he was in subjection to the government of his nation, represented by the king and the princes. In no sense did he preach or practice political subversion or anarchy. Nor did he ever seek to evade or to resist decrees made by the government concerning him, even though these were at times arbitrary and unjust. Yet on the spiritual plane to which God elevated him through his prophetic ministry, Jeremiah exercised authority over the very rulers to whom he was in subjection on the natural plane."[7]

Like Jeremiah, every Christian today has dual citizenship. By natural birth, we are citizens of an earthly nation, subject to its laws. But through spiritual rebirth, we are also citizens of heaven. As such, we are called to declare and decree God's purposes on the earth.

Ministers of Reconciliation

Light overcomes darkness. There is still much darkness in this fallen world. But Jesus has sent you and me to shine His light of love and reconciliation. The apostle Peter tells us of the Father's love for those who are lost in this darkness:

> The Lord is . . . longsuffering toward us, not willing that any should perish but that all should come to repentance (2 Pet. 3:9, *NKJV*).

God desires that all people caught in sin be reconciled to Him. And He has chosen to use the Church as His tool to communicate that love to the world. The apostle Paul speaks of our role as ministers of reconciliation and God's ambassadors:

> Who reconciled us to Himself through Christ and gave us the ministry of reconciliation, namely, that God was

in Christ reconciling the world to Himself, not counting their trespasses against them, and He has committed to us the word of reconciliation. Therefore, we are ambassadors for Christ, as though God were making an appeal through us; we beg you on behalf of Christ, be reconciled to God (2 Cor. 5:18-20).

That is why we pray, "Thy kingdom come." By doing so, we are placing ourselves in agreement with God's plan for the earth (we'll talk more about this in the next chapter). By praying the news, we stand up in the Spirit and declare, "thy will be done" in every issue that we face.

C. S. Lewis referred to this kind of intercessory prayer as being "God's fellow-worker" in the world. "How or why does such faith occur sometimes, but not always, even in the perfect petitioner? . . . My own idea is that it occurs only when the one who prays does so as God's fellow-worker, demanding what is needed for the joint work."

"The difference, we are told, between a servant and a friend is that a servant is not in his master's secrets," Lewis explains. "For him, 'orders are orders.' He has only his own surmises as to the plans he helps to execute. But the fellow-worker, the companion or (dare we say?) the colleague of God is so united with Him at certain moments that something of the divine foreknowledge enters his mind. Hence his faith is the 'evidence'—that it, the evidentness, the obviousness— of things not seen."[8]

When we enter into the ministry of praying the news, we become "God's fellow-worker" in this ministry of reconciliation. Lewis explains that to enter into intercession is to go from being a suitor—one who prays on his own behalf—to being a true servant of the Lord. Lewis goes on to say that it is no sin to be a suitor. "Our Lord descends into the humiliation of being a suitor, of praying on His own behalf, in Gethsemane," he says. "But the vast majority of the time, Jesus, who is our example, plays the part of the servant, interceding for others."[9]

This intercession is part of the priesthood ministry of Jesus that continues to this day:

But He, because He continues forever, has an unchangeable priesthood. Therefore He is also able to save to the uttermost those who come to God through Him, since He always lives to make intercession for them (Heb. 7:24-25, *NKJV*).

God invites us to join with Him in this ministry of reconciliation. And we too have a role to play as priests before God—standing as representatives of fallen man, crying out to heaven for mercy:

> But you are a chosen generation, a royal priesthood, a holy nation, His own special people, that you may proclaim the praises of Him who called you out of darkness into His marvelous light (1 Pet. 2:9, *NKJV*).

> But they shall be priests of God and of Christ, and shall reign with Him a thousand years (Rev. 20:6, *NKJV*).

As we pray God's will on the earth, we are standing as a priest—or an intermediary—between God and man. This is why we pray the news. God's intention from the beginning of time is that we would carry His delegated authority (more on that in the next chapter). So when we are praying "Thy will be done," we are standing in the gap between a holy God and sinful mankind. That is what intercession is all about. C. S. Lewis stated:

> "Thy will be done." But a great deal of it is to be done by God's creatures; including me. The petition, then, is not merely that I may patiently suffer God's will but also that I may vigorously do it. I must be an agent as well as a patient. I am asking that I may be enabled to do it.[10]

An Example of Praying the Good News

So how do we "do" the will of God by praying the news? Many Christians become frustrated, angry, and even overwhelmed when watching or reading the news. But there is a way to pray for the issues and people we see in the news without losing our joy. It comes first by surrendering to God's will as He leads us into this ministry of reconciliation, and then by following the leading of the Holy Spirit when we pray.

"I'm inclined to cancel the newspaper," writer Karen O'Connor told her husband one morning as she leafed through the daily pages.

"I know what you mean," her husband responded, shaking his head as he read the headline of one story after another:

"Local Man Killed While Jogging Before Dawn"
"Drug Bust at the Border"
"Child Run Down by Drunken Driver"

In the same paper, however, were inspiring stories of a father who donated his kidney to his child, a woman honored for 50 years of volunteer service to the local school system, a family who had taken in foster children with disabilities. These and other articles focused on selfless men and women who were making a positive difference in the lives of others.

Where do we draw the line, Karen wondered. "I wanted to stay connected to my community, to the national scene, to global issues, as well. But the 'bad' news seemed to outweigh the good news by a wide margin. And I often left the breakfast table feeling burdened by the crime and hatred I read about. I wondered how I might strike a balance. As a Christian I felt an obligation to read and watch the news so that I can arm myself against deception and stay alert to what is going on in the world in which I live. On the other hand I didn't want to submit myself to the lure of evil or the advertising of false values that is so rampant in our culture."

Paul's words to the Romans came to Karen as she wrestled with what to do next.

Do not conform any longer to the pattern of this world, but be transformed by the renewing of your mind. Then you will be able to test and approve what God's will is—his good, pleasing and perfect will (Rom. 12:2, *NIV*).

Karen decided to "renew" her mind by eliminating the salacious and sensational news stories and focusing, instead, on those articles that uplifted her spirit and fed her mind. "Certainly this new plan saved me a lot of time. I went through the entire paper in a matter of moments!"

"Then one day several months later, I attended a workshop called 'Practicing the Presence of God' at a Christian conference. Author and speaker Jan Johnson, who had written a book on the subject, presented a viewpoint that completely changed the way I now approach the daily news. She shared with the audience a habit she had been developing over time: praying for people in the news—as the Lord leads. I remember how startled I was by this simple spiritual tool that I had completely overlooked. I also saw in that moment of clarity how self-serving I had been up to that point. Instead of engaging in the battle with prayer, I walked away from it. I left the conference with a new commitment to pray daily for the gift of discernment in all my affairs."

Karen decided to take up Jan's challenge. That very week she began reading the paper in an entirely new way, praying for individuals by name, as the Holy Spirit led her. She did not take on the burden of every oppressive detail. Instead, she simply held up the name of the person in need, asking God to make Himself known in that person's life.

"Dear Lord, please touch Mr. Smith with your healing hand."

"God, I feel overwhelmed by R.J.'s evil actions against those little children. Please rescue this boy and girl, and bring R.J. to repentance."

Then she moved on.

"The next day I might be drawn to pray for a man convicted of murder. Another day I might pause and pray over the name of a city official. Sometimes I was moved to pray for an entire family or even a city of people who had been ravaged by a flood or earthquake."

Reading the daily newspaper became an event Karen looked forward to for an entirely new reason. Instead of spending her energy criticizing other people's sin and setting herself above the masses, she realized anew that but for the grace of God, she might be in the pages of that very paper for her own sins!

"I began praying in earnest—thanking God for what He had done in my life and asking for that same gift for others. Today, instead of gossiping about the news, my husband and I pray over it. Instead of condemning the sinners, we come against the sin. Instead of judging the unrighteous, we ask God to release His grace. And what a difference this practice has made in our lives."

Pray in Power and Compassion

So often in the ministry of Jesus, we see where He was moved with compassion for the hurting people He saw all around Him. And when He moved on their behalf, He did so in the power of the Holy Spirit. God wants to give us that same compassion and power. This world is in desperate need of faith-filled Christians to rise up and pray the news.

Are you ready to begin a tremendous adventure in God? The world needs faith-filled believers like you to rise up and intercede that God's will be done and that Satan's plans would be thwarted. It all begins by understanding why we pray, and then recognizing the authority that God has given to us in our prayers. Do you hear God's call to pray the news? Keep reading to learn how!

2

KNOWING YOUR
AUTHORITY IN PRAYER

It was one of the darkest moments during World War II. In May 1940, the Nazis had trapped 400,000 British and French troops between the cliffs and the sea, at Dunkirk on France's north coast. If those troops had been killed or captured, Britain would have fallen to the Germans. All of Europe would have been under the iron rule of the Nazis before the United States even entered into World War II.

At this critical time, God raised up a man named Rees Howells of the Bible College of Wales to lead intercession in Britain. Howells took the initiative to organize nightly intercessory prayer meetings with his students. He instructed them, "God will not do a bit more through you than you have faith for. . . . You are more responsible for this victory today than those men on the battlefield." He added, "I feel tonight that whatever the Nazis do, they cannot escape the Holy Spirit."[1] Soon, prayer meetings were being held across Great Britain in response to Howells's leadership.

Howells's group poured out their hearts to God for hours every day, and soon much of the nation joined in. Parliament recognized the need for God's intervention and called for a national day of prayer. Suddenly, there was a change in the course of the war. Instead of wiping out the troops as he could have, Hitler held his army back, content to bomb Dunkirk instead. During that time, ships, yachts and even rowboats evacuated 338,000 troops across the English Channel—as the water remained miraculously calm. Hitler's behavior made no military sense. It was clear that God had intervened in response to the prayers of believers.

From the Battle of Dunkirk, says author Peter Lundell, "through all the years of the war the whole College was in prayer every evening from seven o'clock to midnight with only a brief interval for supper. They never missed a day. This was in addition to an hour's prayer meeting every morning and very often at midday."[2] Morning, noon and night, all through the war, they never missed a night.

Four months later, during the Battle of Britain, the German Luftwaffe was overpowering Britain's outnumbered Royal Air Force. Great Britain once again faced the terrifying threat of Nazi invasion as Hitler prepared to rule all of Europe. Hope seemed lost, but not to Rees Howells and his students. It was said of him that "faith would stand to the claim and lay hold of the victory; and there would be no rest until he had God's own assurance that faith had prevailed and victory was certain."[3]

The British seemed to be at the point of certain defeat when, suddenly and without explanation, the German planes moved east. The fighting ended as the Luftwaffe, with the potential of victory in hand, turned back for the continent. There is no earthly explanation for why Hitler called off the fight. But Lundell believes the heavenly explanation is obvious: "I do not believe I overstate when I say Rees Howells and his students deserve great credit for Britain being saved and thus turning the tide of the whole European war."[4]

It was the faith-filled prayers of Howells and his students—and then thousands across Britain—that made the difference in the spirit realm. And the spirit realm is where it really counts. Through the prophet Zechariah the Holy Spirit declared:

"Not by might nor by power, but by My Spirit," says the LORD of hosts (Zech. 4:6, *NKJV*).

As disciples of Jesus Christ, our warfare is not against other people. Paul declared, "For we do not wrestle against flesh and blood, but against principalities, against powers, against the rulers of the darkness of this age, against spiritual hosts of wickedness in the heavenly places" (Eph. 6:12, *NKJV*).

God wants to enter the affairs of man and bring answers and solutions to the daunting problems we face. But He is waiting on people of faith to decide to partner with Him in prayer.

While this is a true, biblical statement, have you ever wondered why He would choose to work that way? Why doesn't God just come in and do what He wants to do in the world? He is sovereign, isn't He? He is all-powerful, isn't He?

Why do we need to pray?

The answer to that question is vital to our walking in the full authority that God intends for us to have in prayer.

Exercising Our God-Given Authority in Prayer

To understand the authority that God intends for all believers to exercise, first we need to recognize that all authority resides with God. He is sovereign. He holds the universe in His hands. Anything that exists is there because He willed it to be so. Speaking of the authority of Christ, Paul wrote to the Colossian church:

> For by him [Jesus] all things were created: things in heaven and on earth, visible and invisible, whether thrones or powers or rulers or authorities; all things were created by him and for him. He is before all things, and in him all things hold together (Col. 1:16-17, NIV).

As Creator, God has all authority in heaven and on earth. He can do whatever He desires to do, whenever and wherever He desires to do it.

But the Bible also reveals that God is love. It's important to understand that it is not just that God "loves," but that He is the embodiment of love. Because God is love, He gave a free will to man when he was created.

Then, in a celestial move that surely puzzled the angels, God entrusted mankind with delegated authority on the earth. Then God said, "Let Us make man in Our image, according to Our likeness; let them have dominion" (Gen. 1:26, NKJV).

In what is known as the Edenic Covenant, God gave dominion to man and made him His regent, or ambassador, on the earth to oversee His creation for Him. God gave man responsibility in the world—dominion, or delegated authority—to tend it, to name the animals and to carry out God's will on this planet. Adam and Eve lived in harmonious relationship with God, walking with Him in the cool of the day. They were free to do anything, to have anything, to be anything they wanted to be. They were free to eat of any tree in the garden except the tree of the knowledge of good and evil.

God gave mankind the freedom to choose. Tragically, the man and the woman chose to blatantly rebel against the rule of God. As a result, they lost the dominion that God had given them, becoming slaves of sin and of their own fleshly desires—and Satan became the god (small *g*) of this world. So, for a season, mankind was completely separated from relationship with God by sin, and the devil went basically unchecked in the world, blinding the eyes of man and stirring up rebellion.

But then God sent Jesus to take upon Himself the punishment for man's betrayal. In dying on the cross and rising again from the grave, Jesus took back from Satan the dominion on the earth. In the book of Revelation, Jesus says of Himself, "I was dead, and behold, I am alive forevermore, and I have the keys of death and of Hades" (Rev. 1:18).

Before He ascended into heaven, Jesus told His disciples, "All authority has been given to Me in heaven and on earth" (Matt. 28:18). Jesus was making it clear that as the Son of God, He had all authority in heaven. And because He was the Son of Man who had paid the price of sin on the cross, He now had all authority on earth as well. The Bible calls Jesus the Second Adam, and He received the authority that God had intended for man since the creation.

Through the cross, God established this New Covenant between Himself and man with Christ serving as the Mediator. Jesus as the Son of God represents the Trinity in this Covenant. And then Jesus as the Son of Man represents humankind as well. Because Jesus never sinned and never will sin—unlike the children of Israel who broke the Sinaitic Covenant in their sinful failures to uphold their responsibilities to obey—the New Covenant is everlasting in Christ.

Because it is an everlasting covenant, sealed in the shed blood of Jesus, we are secure in Christ. Believers are then grafted into the family of God as spiritual Israel. Therefore, all of the Old Testament promises of God are yes to those who have faith in Christ: "For in him every one of God's promises is a 'Yes.' For this reason it is through him that we say the 'Amen,' to the glory of God" (2 Cor. 1:20, *NRSV*).

Because of this Covenant, God calls us to partner with Him in prayer that His kingdom would come and His will be done, on earth as it is in heaven. Going back to Matthew 28, after Jesus declares that He has all authority, He then tells His disciples to go into all the world and make disciples. We call this the Great Commission—and this mandate is given to every believer for all time, until Jesus returns.

I (Craig) used to read this passage and think, *Well, it's great that Jesus has all authority, but what about me? He's sending us out to make disciples, but what authority do we have?* Then one day the Lord led me to this passage in Romans that speaks of how God sees us as His children:

> The Spirit Himself testifies with our spirit that we are children of God, and if children, heirs also, heirs of God and fellow heirs with Christ, if indeed we suffer with Him so that we may also be glorified with Him (Rom. 8:16-17).

The term "fellow heirs" or "joint heirs" is a legal term that means that whatever one of the heirs has, all of the other children receive as well. Wow! Because of our covenant with God by faith in Christ, we receive the same authority that Jesus has on the earth. That is why Jesus declared:

> Truly, truly, I say to you, he who believes in Me, the works that I do, he will do also; and greater works than these he will do; because I go to the Father (John 14:12).

It is in Christ, and by His Spirit, that this is possible.

Power in the Name of Jesus

While our prayers can literally change headlines and history, they can also help save lives.

Although it had been only three months since Hurricane Katrina hit New Orleans, Bourbon Street was alive with partiers, revelers and the usual fortune-tellers. I (Wendy) was in town to do a follow-up story on the storm, and my hotel happened to be right in the middle of the "party." It was late, and I was in the mood for something sweet, so I went next door to the diner and ordered a piece of chocolate cake and a peppermint tea.

Minutes later, a young man who was sitting in a booth next to the window yelled, "Call 9-1-1!" I was expecting gunfire to ring out and was ready to get under my seat. Instead, there was a lady with long curly blonde hair sitting next to him, and she wasn't breathing. She wasn't making any choking noises, but she couldn't speak either. My heart started pounding. Several men in uniform came into the restaurant and gathered around her. They could do nothing but stare. I remember thinking, *I need to get up and pray for that woman,* but I almost felt paralyzed by fear. What if they say no? What if my prayer doesn't help? Nevertheless, I knew I had to try. After all, I believed that Jesus healed the sick and in His name we can cast out demons.

Spirit of Infirmity, Come Out!

Somehow, my legs began to move toward the circle of people gathered around the lady's booth. I asked the man who was with her if I could pray for the woman. I watched in astonishment as I saw his mouth form a no, but then it changed into a yes. She still wasn't breathing. I put my hand on her back and prayed quietly, "Lord, please heal this woman." Nothing happened. I rubbed her back, "Lord, bring Your healing power to this woman." Still nothing. I began to think, *Lord, this would be a really good time for You to show up.* Then, I prayed, "In the name of Jesus, spirit of infirmity, come out!" The woman immediately threw up—a lot! She continued to throw up for a while. But she was breathing again. Everything was going to be okay.

The Lord showed up and rescued this woman from possible death. A few minutes later, paramedics arrived with a stretcher and she was taken to the hospital. When I left the diner, the mâitre d' said with a very relieved look on his face, "Thank you."

Once on the street, I saw one of the Louisiana State policemen who had been in the circle around the woman. He said, "You're the lady who prayed?" I said, "Yes." He replied, "I'm a believer too, and I was praying right along with you."

That night in my hotel room, I got down on my knees next to my bed and thanked the Lord for what He did and for using me in such a powerful way to save a woman's life. He spoke to me so tenderly and clearly: *You're going to be doing a lot more of this.*

I was reminded that although sometimes we are sick from natural causes, sometimes it is a demonic spirit that makes someone sick. In his book *The Beginner's Guide to Intercessory Prayer,* Dutch Sheets told the story of a woman who was paralyzed from the neck down for two years for no apparent medical reason. The Holy Spirit prompted his friend that the cause was demonic. So, he knelt beside her wheelchair and prayed, "Satan, I break your hold over this young lady, in the name of Jesus. I command you to lose your hold over her and let her go." There was no immediate healing manifestation as I experienced with the woman in the diner. Yet, a week later, this lady began to move a little; and within a month, she was totally healed and freed from the paralysis that had bound her.[5]

The name of Jesus heals, delivers and sets free today just as it did more than 2,000 years ago. "The Son of God appeared for this purpose, to destroy the works of the devil" (1 John 3:8).

Emmanuel: God with Us

In the New Covenant, God's Spirit dwells within every born-again believer as Emmanuel, God with us. That is why Jesus told His disciples, "Among those born of women there has not arisen anyone greater than John the Baptist! Yet the one who is least in the kingdom of heaven is greater than he" (Matt. 11:11).

Jesus was speaking of us as being greater than the greatest of all Old Testament prophets because we have the Spirit of God dwelling on the inside of us. This is the kind of relationship that God wanted with mankind from the beginning. As joint heirs with Jesus Christ, by faith, we have this delegated authority to be, as we quoted C. S. Lewis earlier, "God's fellow-worker" in the world. That is why the apostle John said of all believers, "As He is, so also are we in this world" (1 John 4:17).

While we receive the Spirit of God as a result of our salvation—we call this "justification"—all believers are on a journey where they are being transformed in their soul (mind, will and emotions) to be like Jesus—which is called "sanctification." Therefore, becoming more and more like Christ is the goal of every Bible-believing Christian, "until we all attain to the unity of the faith, and of the knowledge of the Son of God, to a mature man, to the measure of the stature which belongs to the fullness of Christ" (Eph. 4:13).

So if we are to be Christlike on the earth, and God's purpose is supposed to be ours, then it is important for us to understand what His plan is. God wants to do away with the dominion of darkness and set free those who have been in bondage to sin, to Satan and to their own fleshly desires. As a loving Father, God's objective is to reconcile sinful mankind to Himself, and to crush the works of the devil. We see where God first declared this purpose after the fall of Adam and Eve in Genesis 3:

> I will put enmity between you and the woman, and between your seed and her seed; He shall bruise you on the head, and you shall bruise him on the heel (v. 15).

This promise was partially fulfilled through Jesus on the cross. Scripture tells us that Jesus "canceled the record that contained the charges against us. He took it and destroyed it by nailing it to Christ's cross. In this way, God disarmed the evil rulers and authorities. He shamed them publicly by his victory over them on the cross of Christ" (Col. 2:14-15, NLT).

So, if Jesus defeated Satan on the cross, what is there left for us to do? Why didn't all evil end on earth when Jesus rose from the dead? If the ministry of Jesus on the earth ushered in the kingdom of God, why did He teach us to pray, "Thy kingdom come"?

While the Bible doesn't give us the complete answer to this question, it does give us some clues as to God's reason for how and why He is working in the Church Age—the time since Jesus' death and resurrection. During Jesus' earthly ministry, before He went to the cross, He sent out the 70 disciples in His name and made this significant declaration over them:

> I saw Satan fall like lightning from heaven. Behold, I give you the authority to trample on serpents and scorpions, and over all the power of the enemy, and nothing shall by any means hurt you (Luke 10:18-19, *NKJV*).

This is a direct reference back to God's promise in Genesis 3 to crush the serpent under the heel of the Messiah. But we see here that Jesus has included the disciples in casting Satan down and trampling on serpents and scorpions in His name—obviously referring to the demonic realm. The Lord's intention for us is that we co-labor with Him in defeating the devil and setting the captives free. We see this even more clearly in Paul's admonition to the Romans:

> I want you to be wise in what is good and innocent in what is evil. The God of peace will soon *crush Satan under your feet* (Rom. 16:19-20, emphasis added).

We are co-workers with Christ in overcoming the work of Satan in the earth and shining the light of the gospel to those who are lost in darkness. The Bible calls this the ministry of reconciliation:

> Now all these things are from God, who reconciled us to Himself through Christ and gave us the ministry of reconciliation, namely, that God was in Christ reconciling the world to Himself, not counting their trespasses against them, and

He has committed to us the word of reconciliation. Therefore, we are ambassadors for Christ, as though God were
making an appeal through us; we beg you on behalf of
Christ, be reconciled to God (2 Cor. 5:18-20).

According to *Fausset's Bible Dictionary*, the Greek word for "reconciliation" here is *katallagee*, which means "atonement, sacrifice,
or propitiation."[6] Another way of understanding the concept of
reconciliation is to pronounce the definition as "at-one-ment"
with God—instead of being separated by sin, God has reunited us
to Himself by the sacrifice of Jesus Christ on the cross—making us
"at-one" with Him!

Fausset's Bible Dictionary explains that God has "restored us
(the world, 2 Corinthians 5:19) to His favor by satisfying the claims
of justice against us. The time (aorist) is completely past, imply-
ing a once for all accomplished fact. Our position judicially in the
eye of God's law is altered, not as though Christ's sacrifice made
a change in God's character and made Him to love us. . . . Christ's
sacrifice was the provision of God's love, not its procuring cause.
Christ's blood was the ransom or price paid at God's own cost to
reconcile the exercise of His mercy with justice, not as separate,
but as the eternally co-existing harmonious attributes in the unchangeable God."[7]

Reconciling (*katallassoon*) "implies 'changing' the judicial sta-
tus from one of condemnation to one of justification. The 'at-one-
ment' or reconciliation is the removal of the bar to peace and
acceptance with the holy God, which His righteousness interposed
against our sin. The first step towards peace between us and God
was on God's side (John 3:16). The change now to be effected must
be on the part of offending man, God the offended One being
already reconciled. Man, not God, now needs to be reconciled by
laying aside his enmity against God (Rom. 5:10-11). Ministers' en-
treaty to sinners, 'be ye reconciled to God,' is equivalent to 'receive
the reconciliation' already accomplished."[8]

So our role and responsibility as ambassadors and ministers of
reconciliation will continue until Christ returns and the devil is

completely defeated. As many have said, our responsibility as Christians is "to know Him, and to make Him known." Our calling as disciples of Jesus Christ is to walk daily in a loving relationship with Him, and from that relationship, carry the ministry of reconciliation to those who are lost in darkness.

Along with the authority given to us by Jesus to carry out this Great Commission, God also gives us His revealed Word in the Bible, and the powerful weapon of prayer.

That is why we pray the news.

A Sure Victory

God's Word assures us that the devil will be utterly defeated in the end and Christ will reign as King of kings and Lord of lords. But until that day comes, we are in a spiritual battle. That is why Paul calls us to put on the armor of God: "Put on the full armor of God, so that you will be able to stand firm against the schemes of the devil" (Eph. 6:11).

Paul then encourages us to stand in faith without wavering: "Therefore, take up the full armor of God, so that you will be able to resist in the evil day, and having done everything, to stand firm" (Eph. 6:13).

We are called to be God's co-laborers in this celestial battle for the souls of mankind. As we cooperate with the Spirit of God in this warfare, the devil will be defeated: "And they overcame him because of the blood of the Lamb and because of the word of their testimony, and they did not love their life even when faced with death" (Rev. 12:11).

So this is how Satan is overcome:

- *By the blood of the Lamb*—this was the original defeat of Satan when Jesus died on the cross and took the keys of death and hell from him;

- *By the word of our testimony*—this is the Word of God spoken from our lips both in prayer and in declaration to the evil principalities and powers of darkness;

- *Loving not our life, even unto death*—Jesus taught His disciples, "Unless a grain of wheat falls into the earth and dies, it remains alone; but if it dies, it bears much fruit" (John 12:24). We overcome the devil and walk in the fullness of the fruitful Christian life when we die to our own plans and desires and follow completely the leading of the Holy Spirit and the will of the Father. This is what it means to make Jesus the Lord of your life.

As we surrender to the Lordship of Jesus Christ, we can praise Him in all things! We don't have to despair when we see world events on the news. Instead, we can rejoice because we know these things:

- God is at work reconciling sinful mankind to Himself.
- Satan is already defeated.
- The Lord is using us to see His kingdom established and His will done in the earth.

Waging War with the Word

One of the most powerful weapons we have in the earth is the declaration of the Word of God, both in prayer and in our daily conversation. God created the tongue to be a powerful weapon that can be used both for good and for evil. Scripture says, "Death and life are in the power of the tongue, and those who love it will eat its fruit" (Prov. 18:21). Man has tremendous power in the spirit realm when he speaks or prays the Word of God in faith:

For the word of God is living and active and sharper than any two-edged sword, and piercing as far as the division of soul and spirit, of both joints and marrow, and able to judge the thoughts and intentions of the heart (Heb. 4:12).

We have this power over the enemy in prayer and in our speech because God's Word is a mighty weapon. But we also have power because we are "Sons of Adam" and "Daughters of Eve," as C. S.

Lewis put it in his masterpiece *The Lion, The Witch, and The Wardrobe*. As we've already established, God gave dominion to man in the Edenic Covenant. Because we have an "earth suit" as human beings, we walk in this Edenic Covenant authority. No other creature on the planet has the same authority. No angel or demon has been given this authority. That is why demons want to "possess" a human being, because without an "earth suit," they can do nothing but whisper into the ears of people to deceive.

The authority given to man in the earth, through the Edenic Covenant, has never been revoked. That is why our words have so much power—especially as parents and leaders. When we receive Christ as Savior and Lord, that authority is super-charged and we take a quantum leap forward through the New Covenant. We see this concept explained in the parable of the vineyard:

> A man planted a vineyard and rented it out to vine-growers, and went on a journey for a long time. At the harvest time he sent a slave to the vine-growers, so that they would give him some of the produce of the vineyard; but the vine-growers beat him and sent him away empty-handed. And he proceeded to send another slave; and they beat him also and treated him shamefully and sent him away empty-handed. And he proceeded to send a third; and this one also they wounded and cast out.
>
> The owner of the vineyard said, "What shall I do? I will send my beloved son; perhaps they will respect him." But when the vine-growers saw him, they reasoned with one another, saying, "This is the heir; let us kill him so that the inheritance will be ours." So they threw him out of the vineyard and killed him.
>
> What, then, will the owner of the vineyard do to them? He will come and destroy these vine-growers and will give the vineyard to others (Luke 20:9-16).

Planet Earth is the vineyard that God planted in this parable. He leased this planet out to mankind when He gave us dominion over everything that lives here. In our sin, man shunned and even killed God's messengers, the Old Testament prophets. Then when God sent His Son, we crucified Him. But in His mercy, and through the shed blood of Jesus on the cross, the owner of the vineyard has extended the dominion in the earth to all who would receive Jesus as Lord and Savior.

God remains sovereign, but He has given mankind permission to run things on the earth. That is why Scripture declares: "The earth is the LORD's, and all it contains, the world, and those who dwell in it" (Ps. 24:1).

But the Bible also says, "The earth He has given to the sons of men" (Ps. 115:16). Some have called these two Scriptures a contradiction. But the parable of the vineyard shows that these are actually what we call "truths in tension." God is the owner of the vineyard, and He has leased it out to man during this parenthesis in eternity that we call "time."

It's like this: If a person owns an apartment building and leases out one of the units, that person remains the owner of the entire building—including the dwelling being rented. But at the same time, the person who leases the apartment can rightfully and legally say, "This is my home." Because the person has signed a lease, he can arrange the furniture any way he wants, hang pictures on the walls and stay up until any hour of the night. If he has the stipulation in his lease, he can even paint the walls another color. This is the arrangement that God has made with us. He is sovereign, so the earth is His possession. But in His plan of love, He has delegated authority on the earth to man.

We see an interesting Old Testament picture of the authority of Christ and the dominion of man in the book of Daniel:

> I kept looking in the night visions, and behold, with the clouds of heaven One like a Son of Man was coming, and He came up to the Ancient of Days and was presented before Him. And to Him was given dominion, glory and a kingdom, that all the peoples, nations and men of every language might serve Him. His dominion is an everlasting

dominion which will not pass away; and His kingdom is one which will not be destroyed (Dan. 7:13-14).

Daniel then says that his spirit was troubled at this vision. I believe it was because his vision was revealing the Father (the Ancient of Days) giving all authority to Christ (One like a Son of Man). As a Jew, Daniel would have been greatly troubled because their paradigm was that God is One. As Christians, we also believe that God is One, but that He is revealed in three persons—Father, Son and Holy Spirit. I believe that Daniel was seeing the distinction between Father and Son in this vision.

We receive further explanation of God's delegated authority as Daniel continues:

But the saints of the Highest One will receive the kingdom and possess the kingdom forever, for all ages to come (Dan. 7:18).

I kept looking, and that horn was waging war with the saints and overpowering them until the Ancient of Days came and judgment was passed in favor of the saints of the Highest One, and the time arrived when the saints took possession of the kingdom (Dan. 7:21-22).

Here we see the spiritual warfare between Satan and the saints—the Hebrew word is *qaddish*, which means "holy ones." But God intervenes, and we see that "the saints took possession of the kingdom." I believe this is referring to our ministry as co-laborers with Christ in reconciling the world to God.

The vision continues, and we see a clear picture of the saints sharing dominion as joint heirs in the earth:

He [Satan] will speak out against the Most High and wear down the saints of the Highest One . . . But the court will sit for judgment, and his dominion will be taken away, annihilated and destroyed forever. Then the sovereignty, the dominion and the greatness of all the kingdoms under the whole heaven will be *given to the people of the saints of the Highest One;* His kingdom will be an everlasting kingdom, and *all the dominions will serve and obey Him* (Dan. 7:25-27, emphasis added).

The term "Highest One" here is the Hebrew name for God Most High, or *El Elyon.* We see here that Satan and his servants are fighting against God and His holy ones. But the devil's dominion is taken away and given to the saints of God. This is the delegated authority we walk in as joint heirs with Jesus Christ.

Then immediately we see where the Kingdom of God is described as an everlasting kingdom, where all the dominions, including the delegated authority we walk in, will serve and obey Him. This is the Kingdom of God that Jesus preached and that He instructed us to pray for. The word "kingdom" literally means "the dominion of the king." *Fausset's Dictionary* defines it as: "Messiah's kingdom, as a whole, both in its present spiritual invisible phase . . . and also in its future manifestation on earth in glory, when finally heaven and earth shall be joined."[9]

Walking in this authority in prayer is the restoration of the dominion that God gave to man in the Garden, which is delegated authority under submission to the sovereignty of God. It is under the dominion given to us in both the Edenic and the New Covenants that we walk in as co-laborers and joint heirs with God in prayer, declaring, "Your kingdom come, Your will be done, on earth as it is in heaven" (Matt. 6:10). It is to this end and with this authority that God calls us to pray the news.

3

UNDERSTANDING THE NEWS

Nancy was a journalist in the mainstream media in the 1980s. At the time, she was a part of a Wednesday night prayer group at an evangelical church. One woman in the group was particularly concerned with the negative press that President Ronald Reagan was receiving in the media. She was sitting next to Nancy in a prayer circle one night when she began to pray that "the yapping dogs of the press" would stand down and leave the president alone.

"I had a hard time keeping from laughing out loud," Nancy explains, "because at the time, I worked for Dow Jones, editing the *Wall Street Journal*. I don't think she knew where I worked. Yet I was also somewhat annoyed because of her assumption—and that of many other Christians—that the media is an entirely secular industry peopled by "yapping dogs" with no personal faith or conscience, or any right to an opinion that differed from hers.

"After the prayer time concluded, I couldn't help myself," Nancy remembers. "I leaned over to her with a smile and said, 'You know, Diane [not her real name], I'm one of those yapping dogs.' She froze for a moment and then began to stammer, not knowing how to respond. I'm not a mean person, so I let her off the hook, explaining where I worked. Even though the *Journal* was known for its conservative views, I understood her feelings of frustration with the often-liberal media.

"We laughed a little over the incident. But she managed to get away from me pretty quickly, and I don't think she ever sat next to me in a prayer meeting again."[1]

As we enter into intercession for the media, we need to remember that those who work in the field of journalism are just people, like you and me, who need Jesus and have a need to be loved. Many of them are good-hearted people who truly want to help others.

In their zeal to uphold the truth, some Christians may neglect to walk in grace and love when interacting with the media. They forget that Jesus came in "grace and truth" (John 1:14) and that we are supposed to be like Him in all that we do. The truth Jesus spoke was always delivered in a spirit of grace and love. Too often, Christians today confront the media with what they see as truth, but they do not walk in the grace and love of Jesus, and so they sound like a "noisy gong or a clanging cymbal" (1 Cor. 13:1) to those they wish to influence.

"If I reported on the abortion issue," veteran TV news anchor Scott Baker explains, "I would get people calling in to complain about that story. If I got ten calls, five were from people who were pro-choice, and five were from people who were pro-life. Usually the pro-choice people were relatively polite and had a factual problem with some aspect of the story. Almost universally, the conservatives were abysmally behaved. They hadn't really watched the story. They just assumed that I was a secular idiot, and they wanted to tell me that."

Scott tells how, in one city, there was a liberal talk show host who was asked to be a guest speaker at an evening event at his church. "I couldn't go to this debate because I was working at the station. But I knew the woman organizing it. It started at seven o'clock, and she called me at 7:15. I said, 'Did nobody show up?' She answered, 'No, there are a couple hundred people here.' I asked, 'Why aren't you in the meeting'? She replied, 'I'm so embarrassed at the behavior of the people in the church that I had to leave the room.'"

"I found that to be the case a lot of the time," Baker laments, "very abusive behavior by Christians toward people in the media. And if it wasn't abusive, it was extraordinarily condescending. And that doesn't work for anybody."

God wants us to be His ambassadors of love to this hurting world. It is significant that the apostle John, under the influence of the Holy Spirit, wrote that Jesus came in "grace" first, and then in "truth." I can be full of knowledge, but if I don't share that knowledge in a spirit of grace, humility and love, it will profit me nothing (see 1 Cor. 13). Instead, our goal must be to walk in grace and love first, and then speak truth from that humble place. As the apostle Paul wrote, "But speaking the truth in love, we are to grow up in all aspects into Him who is the head, even Christ" (Eph. 4:15).

"As you think about the media and reporters' roles as you are interacting with them," Baker advises, "and as you are praying for them, there needs to be not only a sense of civility, but also, I think, humility. I think that this will bring you a much greater sense of interaction and accomplishment."

In order for any of us to truly love someone, we need to seek to understand who the person is and what motivates him to do what he does. In order to understand those who work in the news media, we need to understand the field of journalism and its place in our society.

News Media—The Fourth Estate

Let's start by asking, what is news?

The term "Fourth Estate" was first used in the late eighteenth century to describe the press. The term is attributed to Edmund Burke, a member of the British Parliament, in a debate on opening up the House of Commons to newspaper reporters. In his book *On Heroes, Hero-Worship and the Heroic in History*, Thomas Carlyle wrote, "Burke said there were Three Estates in Parliament; but, in the Reporter's Gallery yonder, there sat a Fourth Estate more important far than they all."[2]

Burke would have been making reference to the traditional three estates of Parliament: the Lords Spiritual (the clergy), the Lords Temporal (the nobility) and the Commons (the commoners). Under the American system, the press is considered the "fourth estate" as if to say it is the fourth branch of government, in addition to the executive, legislative and judicial branch. In a representative democracy, and under the United States Constitution, freedom of the press is established as a "check and a balance" to the government.

The Founding Fathers provided freedom of the press as a "watchdog" to keep the government—and the rest of society—accountable for their words and actions. The role of the press in a representative democracy is also to help inform the public so that they can participate in the democratic process and become informed voters.

"In some respect, democracy does depend on good journalism," observes Scott Baker. The responsibility of the press, under the Constitution, is to act as a protector of liberty in a free society.

The Power of the Press

"I wasn't a born-again Christian when I was in the news business," former news director Jim DeSantis explains. "But I still maintained that journalistic integrity, instinctively. There were certain stories that we didn't do—like putting a suicide on the air. You had to do the accidents, and you had to do the fires. That was just part and parcel of the business, because people wanted to know about it. And of course you had the competition there among the stations to have all the late-breaking stories. When you're in a small town, let's face it, those are the big stories.

"As a news director for a local CBS TV affiliate, I could do great harm or great good," DeSantis explains. "It was in my hands. Powerful."

In 1992, I (Wendy) saw the immense power of a news story firsthand. I was the weekend anchor at WCHS TV, an ABC affiliate in Charleston, West Virginia. About a week before state elections, it was revealed to me that one of the candidates for attorney general was believed to be trading legal work for sex. I was able to find several women willing to come forward to testify in great detail that this had happened to them. The story first broke on a Friday night, just four days before the Tuesday election. The democratic candidate, who was considered the front-runner, was outraged.

We invited him to come on the air live during our Sunday night broadcast and defend himself. Instead, he showed his true colors, accusing me of ulterior motives and also threatening to sue the station for $20 million (which he later did). The story went statewide and then nationwide. I had no idea what I had stumbled upon; and because I wasn't yet a born-again Christian, I didn't realize how God was possibly using a very naïve young reporter to literally change the headlines. Essentially, God delivered this story into my hands and almost overnight stopped what appeared to be a very immoral person from becoming the top legal authority in the great state of West Virginia where I was born.

I thank God that He uses us even when we are unaware and seemingly unqualified. I have to believe that many people were praying for me and for the victims during this scandal that rocked our state. By the way, the lawsuit was later dropped, and the candidate was sentenced to federal prison and lost his law license in another scandal related to the West Virginia Lottery, and he never ran for public office again. The Bible says, "God deliberately chose things the world considers foolish in order to shame those who think they are wise. And he chose those who are powerless to shame those who are powerful" (1 Cor. 1:27, *NLT*). I believe that God chose me, weak and powerless, to accomplish His will.

In 1988, Scott Baker produced Chuck Colson's first radio series. "It was called Issues '88," Baker explains. "Through a few church scandals that I saw growing up and working with Chuck, I really started to cement that idea that power does corrupt. And it even corrupts good people. If there is a role for a reporter, there is a check and a balance; it is to not be afraid of the truth, even if it's not pleasant.

"The truth sometimes is noble," Baker continues, "and lovely, and enlightening. But sometimes it's not. And sometimes even in the church, it's not."

Baker recalls a story that brought this home to him. He says, "I've often said that Christian journalism, especially Christian journalism about Christianity, is praying for courage to report things that will be unpopular—things that may lead you to feel condemned by other Christians.

"There was a series that I was working on when I left channel 4 in Pittsburgh and never got to finish it. I had come to realize that a number of very significant church leaders in Pittsburgh were claiming to have not honorary degrees, but actually earned degrees. But they didn't. There are very legitimate online education programs, and then there are online programs that are not. And so you have lots of people running around saying, 'I'm Doctor so-and-so, and I have a degree in counseling and therapy,' and they didn't. And I realized that one of them was actually within my own church. He was highly praised and in leadership roles, and he actually agreed to an interview.

"I said to him, 'Why would you claim this when you know that you didn't earn it?' He admitted that he had been self-deceived over time. He said, 'I did attend a couple of seminars, and I listened to some tapes. I guess I thought what I learned would be helpful.' And I said to him, 'In Pennsylvania, you have to have a license to cut people's hair or to fix your car. So why is caring for people's souls something that you can kind of just play along with just for your own self-aggrandizement so you can sell more books and be a speaker?'

"I realized that if I aired this story about this very visible pastor and the leader of a big business, I was going to be castigated for it. But if I hadn't left the station, I would have gone through with that story.

"So I think that prayers for the courage of Christian journalists are important, too."

Accuracy and Fairness

I (Craig) did a joint-degree in Journalism and Divinity for my Master's Degree at Regent University in Virginia Beach. In my journalism training, I immediately learned the professional ethic that demands accuracy and fairness in reporting. In my undergraduate communication training, I was required to take media courses from which I also learned another foundational ethic: objectivity. These two traditions—accuracy along with fairness, and objectivity—summarize the goal of reporters and editors in the newsroom.

The ethic of accuracy and fairness is a goal that most journalists truly strive to attain. But the definition of what is accurate and what is fair in news reporting differs widely based on one's worldview, political persuasion and frame of reference. So what one reporter from a conservative standpoint would consider as fair and accurate, a liberal reporter might see as completely off base.

The slogan of Fox News is "Fair and Balanced," which reflects these journalistic ethics. But if you were to ask a liberal reporter if Fox News was, in fact, fair and balanced, they might laugh in your face. Now, it's not because Fox News is not fair and balanced—at least from a conservative perspective—it's because the liberal reporter will be judging the fairness and balance of Fox News through his or her worldview and political lens, which is tainted by his/her frame of reference.

One's frame of reference is the viewfinder through which he or she observes the world. So, if someone is a middle-class son of a steelworker from Gary, Indiana, who had to work his way through college and take student loans to cover the difference, he is going to see the world differently from an upper-class son of a banker from Connecticut, who never had to work until after he graduated from Harvard with a law degree. There is nothing right or wrong with either upbringing—we all begin from different places in life. But our journey along the way will shape the way we view the world and how we respond in different situations. This ever-changing window on the world colors our thinking and shapes our values and beliefs.

Because man is finite, knowing only what can be observed, the goal of accuracy and fairness is an ideal that can never be perfectly attained on this earth. Bob Woodward and Carl Bernstein were the reporters from the *Washington Post* who broke the Watergate scandal that brought down the Nixon administration. Woodward was involved in a court case where he was defending an investigative story published by the *Post* where he said of the piece, it was "the best obtainable version of the truth."[3]

The reporter's job is to find and report the facts of the story. But this is not as easy as it sounds. Sometimes the facts are hard to come by. For numerous reasons, individuals and groups sometimes try to hide the truth. At times, people will twist or spin the facts. It is often difficult to interpret what the facts actually mean.

It can be difficult to determine if the information that is gathered is factual at all. It may have an element of truth mixed in with a whole lot of agenda and spin. Or it may be merely the opinion of the source based on his or her political persuasion—and not factual at all.

The pressures of today's 24-7 news environment present even more challenges. Reporters often have only a few hours—or at most, a few days—to gather information on a story. They need to process and interpret that information to determine what is factual and what is not. Then they need to write a story or produce a video piece based on the best information they can find.

This brings us back to the journalistic ethics of accuracy, fairness and objectivity.

Accuracy is the most important element of any news story; but as you can see, it is not always possible. Still, accuracy is the goal of any good journalist. For the sincere and professional reporter, accuracy is essential in every detail. Every name must be spelled correctly; every quote has to repeat what was actually said; every list of numbers must add up. And to be truly accurate, you must also present these details in the proper context.

But the reporter cannot tell what the truth actually is without adding to accuracy the further ethic of fairness.

In reporting the news, the journalist will collect information, quotes and even research and statistics from a number of different sources on any issue. In any news story there will be different viewpoints from which an event or an issue can be observed. And all of the different worldviews and political perspectives will likely give a different interpretation of the meaning behind any particular news story.

The reporter desiring to be fair and balanced will seek to find every leading viewpoint on a story. There are always at least two perspectives, and often three or more. The reporter seeking to be fair will make every effort to tell all sides of the story and avoid following their own bias. This leads us to the second ethic of good journalism: objectivity.

Media Bias

In my (Craig's) senior year in college, I wrote a paper on the concept of objective reporting in journalism. After doing extensive research and reading on the subject, I came to the conclusion that there was no such thing as truly unbiased reporting. I received a B-plus because the professor said that reporters "were required to be unbiased."

In my opinion, this was a classic case of the idealism of academia not being in sync with what is actual reality in the working world. Most journalists and editors have also concluded that true objectivity is impossible. Media magnate Henry Luce, who oversaw the rise of *Time, Life* and *Fortune* magazines, did not believe in the concept of unbiased journalism, but instead suggested that reporters should understand that they must aim for fairness in reporting.

Objectivity has been promoted as an ideal by leaders of the journalism profession even if it is unattainable. But critics, like sociologist Gaye Tuchman, have attacked objectivity as a "strategic ritual" that conceals a multitude of professional sins, while producing superficial and often misleading coverage.[4] Michael Schudson, in his book *Discovering the News,* wrote, "Journalists came to believe in objectivity, to the extent that they did, because they wanted to, needed to, were forced by ordinary human aspiration to seek escape from their own deep convictions of doubt and drift."[5]

CBS News reporter Bernard Goldberg infuriated his fellow liberal journalists when he wrote his book *Bias* in which he described how the liberal view of the TV network executives, producers and reporters colored the way they reported the news. Goldberg, who worked at CBS for 28 years, wrote about how he as a liberal from New York City came to the conclusion that instead of being objective, fair and balanced, the network news, for the most part, leaned heavily to the left.[6]

"When I was in media, it was a closed society," explains Jim DeSantis, a former news director for a local CBS network affiliate. "You had a handful of news directors across the country that were controlling the flow of local news. And the higher up the pyramid you went into the major markets, you had even fewer and fewer hands controlling it. It took integrity to do that."

DeSantis remembers how it was: "The guy that taught me was the old reporter type with the press card in his hat. It was hardcore— you'd better have your facts; you'd better do the five Ws (who, what, where, when and why), and sometimes how; you'd better have your sources verified, or it doesn't get on.

"I had friends who were Republicans and Democrats. Nobody knew what my political affiliation was because I always registered as an Independent. I didn't want anybody to think that my judgment was being skewed by my political leanings. And it never was. That's why I had friends on both sides of the aisle. They knew they could trust me to give their side of the story. Now, if it was obvious 'boloney,' because you do check your facts, then you call them on it. That's what journalists are supposed to do.

"In the 1970s, I began to see that a lot of graduates of the journalism schools were coming out with this attitude of 'I'm going to make a difference with the news.' It became 'advocacy journalism.' But that is not a journalist's job. Your job is to gather the facts from both sides, sometimes three sides, sometimes four sides, and present those facts without adding your own adjectives, if you know what I mean. But that happens now on mainstream media, and it's just ridiculous.

"So advocacy journalism began to take over the newsrooms. I attribute that to the college professors who came out of the 1960s, and this whole anti-government, anti-establishment mentality found its way into the newsroom. It has shifted away from integrity.

"I had that struggle in the newsroom when a couple of people that came out of the advocacy journalism mentality joined my news staff. I was constantly fighting the battle—'You cannot put that on'; 'Who's your source?'—and they would answer, 'I'm not telling you my source.' Well, I'm the news director, and if we get sued, my head's on the block. The story didn't get on because that's not how you do journalism."

DeSantis was born again after he left the news media. I asked him how his relationship with Christ changed his view of journalism.

"It hasn't," DeSantis immediately answered. "Jesus said, 'Render unto Caesar what is Caesar's and unto God what is God's.' You have to look at it from a pragmatic point of view. I don't know the religious views of a Brian Williams or a Diane Sawyer or a Katie

Couric, so I can't judge them based on that criteria. If I knew that Brian Williams was a born-again Christian, then I'd have a serious problem with what he's doing. But I don't know that. So I look at media as 'of the world,' and we as Christians are 'in the world.' We have to judge them based upon what they're producing and what they're telling us. You will know them by their fruit.

"In the first couple of weeks after I was saved, I called my Christian friend and said, 'I don't know what to do now. I'm lost.' He gave me a Ryrie study Bible, which I still often use, and he said, 'This is your new life. Now you're going to have the discernment to know what it means.' I knew what the Bible said; I had debated with him for five years. But I didn't know what it meant. After I was born again, I had the spiritual discernment because I had the Holy Spirit helping me—teaching me.

"When you try to apply this to the media, you can only tell where they are coming from by what their fruits are. So when I judge the media, I do so based on my journalism background, training and experience. I don't judge it spiritually, because we don't know what God's purpose is in all of this."

When praying the news, then, it is important to understand that the bias of journalists will color their reporting, and so we need to watch and read the news with this reality in mind.

Let Truth and Error Grapple

One of the most influential documents defending the principle of the right to freedom of speech and expression is John Milton's *Areopagitica*, which was written in opposition to censorship. In this important declaration, Milton called for freedom of speech and freedom of the press in society, explaining that as falsehood and truth are exposed, truth will always rise to the top:

> And though all the winds of doctrine were let loose to play on the earth, so Truth be in the field, we do injuriously, by licensing and prohibiting, to misdoubt her strength. Let her and Falsehood grapple; who ever knew Truth put to the worse in a free and open encounter? Give me the

liberty to know, to utter, and to argue freely according to conscience, above all liberties.[7]

In his first inaugural address (March 4, 1801), Thomas Jefferson declared, "Error of opinion may be tolerated where reason is left free to combat it."[8] Though there are times when we may be frustrated by the falsehoods that are reported under the bias of certain journalists, if we will allow truth and falsehood to grapple in an atmosphere of freedom of the press and freedom of speech, truth will always win—because in the end, all truth is God's truth.

Media Is Revenue Driven

One of the other concepts that a journalist quickly learns is the reality that all media is revenue driven. The news business is still a business. We need to remember this when praying the news. As a business, any media outlet needs to take in more money than it spends. As a result, journalists have to continually look for stories that will be of interest to the most people possible. This can drive some in the media to feature more sensationalistic stories, because the more people who read a publication or watch a program or log on to a website, the more money they can charge for advertising.

We get a good idea of the financial realities a news organization faces when we look at how a newspaper is organized. Some might think that the priority of a newspaper in the editing process would be the news. But in reality, when a newspaper is laid out by an editor, it is the advertising that is placed first. The space that remains is called the "news hole." Owners often apply pressure on editors and reporters to either find sensational stories or write controversial, or attack, pieces to either sell more newspapers or attract more viewers so they can make more money from advertisers.

When praying the news, we need to recognize the pressures that people in the field of journalism are under and why they are sometimes motivated to run certain stories or fan certain controversies. Instead of speaking ill of journalists, we should pray for them, because God loves them and He wants to turn what seem to be negative stories in the press into something that can be used for His glory.

"Our Lives Are a Prayer"

Now that we understand the motivation of the media and how it works, we are better able to interpret the stories we see. We are also better able to respond to the perceived, or actual, attacks against the Church or individual Christians.

When people become public figures, they place themselves in a position where their words and actions are more highly scrutinized by the media. This is part of the price for being in the public eye. Being a public figure can be both a blessing and a burden. The public exposure can bring opportunities and financial gain. At the same time, a person's reputation can be destroyed and career ruined under the white-hot glare of reporters chasing down a story they believe to be motivated by injustice, greed or arrogance.

Kathie Lee Gifford found herself the victim of just such a media feeding frenzy when her clothing business was linked with sweatshops in impoverished nations.

For 15 years, Kathie Lee was seen by millions of people every day on the TV talk show *Live with Regis and Kathie Lee*, which she co-hosted with Regis Philbin. Her fans were shocked when the news media accused her of running sweatshops. Kathie Lee had licensed her name to a clothing line for Walmart. The clothes were produced at a Honduran plant that abused child labor and a New York factory that had been cited for cheating workers of their wages.

Ironically, the story broke at the same time that Kathie Lee was about to open a $7 million home for AIDS and crack babies in New York City, using the proceeds from this same clothing line. She was stunned by the accusations, as she had been a child advocate her entire life. "To be accused of abusing children was devastating," she said. "I can't even describe how excruciating that was."

But what hurt Kathie the most was that it seemed that there were people who wanted to believe what was being reported by the media. One man even testified before Congress, accusing her of purposely dealing with these sweatshops to increase her own personal wealth. She was stunned that someone could stand up and say, "This woman runs sweatshops," and not be held accountable for that accusation. Three months later, the man publicly apologized to her, but few if any newspapers, magazines or other media outlets covered that part of the story.

Kathie cried out to the Lord for help in the midst of this firestorm of criticism. "I really do believe that the will of God never leads you where the grace of God will not keep you," Kathie declared. For whatever reason, the Lord had allowed this attack against her character to happen, and so she sought guidance to discover what the purpose of the Lord could be.

"I went to meet with the late Cardinal John O'Connor, bishop of the Roman Catholic Archdiocese of New York," Gifford remembers. "After I shared how difficult the last months had been, he tenderly told me something that absolutely changed my life. He said, 'Kathie Lee, our Lord did not change this world so much through His miracles as through His suffering. If you are willing to suffer this injustice for His sake, imagine how you can change the world.'

"His words hit me like a ton of bricks. I realized that I was so focused on my own hurt and despair that I couldn't see that maybe God wanted me to help people by getting involved. My focus on my own pain suddenly seemed very selfish and insignificant to me."

She prayed, "Lord, if this be Your will, teach me. Lord, if You want me here, You have got to show me why, or else I am going to quit. I also bear Your name. I don't want You being dragged into the mud with all of this."

"What I needed was to take my eyes off of me and get my eyes back on the Lord and the real suffering of other people. As bad as I felt going through that time, it was nothing compared to all the anguish and despair of little kids and other people in life who are victims of truly evil people [who are] only focused on making a buck at the end of the day. I got a huge education out of that."

After this, Kathie Lee learned all she could about sweatshops. She testified before Congress on a bill to ban the import of goods produced by child labor. "I ended up working with Congress and President Clinton, and we changed the laws. My president, governor, attorney general and secretary of labor all literally said to me, 'You are the only person who is going to be able to change this.' They told me that sweatshops have been a problem for hundreds of years; but until my name was in the newspapers and people became aware of it, little had been done. Because of the publicity, landmark legislation was passed.

"I don't think I would have had the courage to stand up to this fight if I hadn't known the Lord. The Holy Spirit kicked in and said, *Wait a minute. All things work together for good for those who love God (see Romans 8:28). That means all things—not just that beautiful baby girl you had a couple of years ago—but this crisis as well.* That is the hard walk with the Lord; not the good times, but the tough times, too."

Kathie Lee recognized that what seemed to be an attack from the media could actually be turned into a blessing for countless people if she would humble herself, pray and work to shine the light of truth into the dark world of the sweatshops. "The Bible says to pray without ceasing (see 1 Thess. 5:17). To me that says that our lives are meant to be a prayer. Once I realized that, it changed everything for me."[9]

While some in the media saw this story as an opportunity to attack and possibly destroy someone who had set herself up as a Christian role model, others truly had concern with the plight of those in the sweatshops and desired to see them closed down. By yielding to God's higher purpose, Kathie Lee went from being a victim of a seemingly hostile press to becoming an advocate for the oppressed people in sweatshops around the world.

By God's grace, and with His wisdom, she was able to use this occasion as an opportunity to shine the light of the media spotlight on an area of oppression in the world that needed to be brought out of darkness.

As God's people pray the news—and pray for those who report the news—God can take these negative kinds of stories and turn them for good, just as He did with Kathie Lee Gifford.

The Prophetic Role of the Church

As we have shown, the role of the press is both to inform the public and to act as a watchdog to protect people from abuses from government, in businesses and even in religion. The role of the Church is to pray for God's will to be done in any and every situation. We are to be diligent in our prayer, for we don't know the hour and the day of Christ's return.

> So keep a sharp lookout! For you do not know when the homeowner will return—at evening, midnight, early dawn, or late daybreak (Mark 13:35, *NLT*).

We need to be watching and reading the news with an ear tuned to the voice of the Spirit so that we can "stay alert and keep watch" like the Sons of Issachar, "men who understood the times, with knowledge of what Israel should do" (1 Chron. 12:32).

In the parable of the talents, the Master distributes the resources to the servants before he leaves to go on a journey and declares, "Occupy til I come" (Luke 19:13, *KJV*). Other versions say, "Do business with this until I come back" (*NASB*). God wants His Church to be about His kingdom business, occupying the territory that He has taken from the devil until He returns.

Until the time of Christ's return, we are to be praying for peace in our communities: for justice; for mercy for the poor; and that God's kingdom will be manifest in our cities, states and nation. We are to pray for godly leadership in all areas of society, because "when the righteous increase, the people rejoice, but when a wicked man rules, people groan" (Prov. 29:2).

Spiritual warfare is very real. The stakes couldn't be higher. We are contending in prayer in the spirit realm for the souls of people who are destined for an eternity apart from God unless they come to Christ. And as the apostle Peter warns, "Be of sober spirit, be on the alert. Your adversary, the devil, prowls around like a roaring lion, seeking someone to devour" (1 Pet. 5:8).

There are still many people who are lost in darkness that actually become tools in the hands of the devil to attack the Church and bring injury to innocent people. Again and again in history we see the tug of war between righteous people and those who are manipulated by Satan in his war against God and His people. The psalmist warns:

> For, behold, the wicked bend the bow, they make ready their arrow upon the string to shoot in darkness at the upright in heart. If the foundations are destroyed, what can the righteous do? (Ps. 11:2-3).

Jesus said that on this earth we will have trouble and persecution (see John 16:33; 2 Tim. 3:12). As we saw on September 11, 2001, there are evil forces unleashed in the earth. The thief comes to steal, kill and destroy (see John 10:10). The Church must be diligent in prayer to thwart the plan of the Enemy. Now that we understand how the media works, we can move on to learn how we can be most effective in praying the news.

4

HOW TO PRAY
THE NEWS

The late international Bible expositor Derek Prince saw firsthand how prayer changed circumstances when he was a soldier in the British army stationed in North Africa during World War II.

"For me, the power of prayer to shape history is no mere abstract theological formula. I have seen it demonstrated in my own experience on many occasions. . . . From 1941 to 1943, I served as a hospital attendant with the British forces in North Africa. . . . At that time, the morale of the British forces in the desert was very low. The basic problem was that the men did not have confidence in their officers. I myself am the son of an army officer, and many of the friends with whom I grew up were from the same background. I thus had some valid standards of judgment. As a group, the officers in the desert at that time were selfish, irresponsible, and undisciplined. Their main concern was not the well-being of the men, or even the effective prosecution of the war, but their own physical comfort.

"The result of all this was the longest retreat in the history of the British army—about 700 miles in all—from a place in Tripoli called El Agheila to El Alamein, about 50 miles west of Cairo. Here the British forces dug in for one final stand. If El Alamein should fall, the way would be open for the Axis power to gain control of Egypt, to cut the Suez Canal and to move over into Palestine. The Jewish community there would then be subjected to the same treatment that was already being meted out to the Jews in every area of Europe that had come under Nazi control."[1]

In the desert, Prince had no church or minister to offer him fellowship or counsel. "I was obliged to depend upon the two great basic provisions of God for every Christian: the Bible and the Holy Spirit. I early came to see that, by New Testament standards, fasting was a normal part of Christian discipline. During the whole period that I was in the desert, I regularly set aside Wednesday of each week as a special day for fasting and prayer.

"During the long and demoralizing retreat to the gates of Cairo, God laid on my heart a burden of prayer, both for the British forces in the desert and for the whole situation in the Middle East. Yet I could not see how God could bless leadership that was so unworthy and inefficient. I searched in my heart for some form of prayer that I could pray with genuine faith and that would cover the needs of the situation. After a while, it seemed that the Holy Spirit gave me this prayer: 'Lord, give us leaders such that it will be for Your glory to give us victory through them.'

"I continued praying this prayer every day. In due course, the British government decided to relieve the commander of their forces in the desert and to replace him with another man. The man whom they chose was a general named W. H. E. 'Strafer' Gott. He was flown to Cairo to take over command, but was killed when his plane was shot down. At this critical juncture, the British forces in this major theater of the war were left without a commander. Winston Churchill, then prime minister of Britain, proceeded to act largely on his own initiative. He appointed a more-or-less unknown officer, named B. L. Montgomery, who was hastily flown out from Britain.

"Montgomery was the son of an evangelical Anglican bishop. He was a man who very definitely fulfilled God's two requirements in a leader of men. He was just and God-fearing. He was also a man of tremendous discipline. Within two months, he had instilled a totally new sense of discipline into his officers and had thus restored the confidence of the men in their leaders.

"Then the main battle of El Alamein was fought. It was the first major Allied victory in the entire war up to that time. The threat to Egypt, the Suez Canal, and Palestine was finally thrown back, and the course of the war changed in favor of the Allies. Without a doubt, the battle of El Alamein was the turning point of the war in North Africa.

"Two or three days after the battle, I found myself in the desert a few miles behind the advancing Allied forces. A small portable radio beside me on the tailboard of the military truck was relaying a news commentator's description of the scene at Montgomery's headquarters as he had witnessed it on the eve of the battle. He recalled how Montgomery publicly called his officers and men to prayer, saying, 'Let us ask the Lord, mighty in battle, to give us the victory.' As these words came through that portable radio, God spoke very clearly to my spirit, 'That is the answer to your prayer.' "[2]

This critical change in leadership helped change the course of the entire war. The British government chose Gott for their commander, but God had another plan and raised up Montgomery. By this intervention, God also preserved the Jews in Palestine from coming under the control of the Nazi invaders.

Prince wrote, "I believe that the prayer that God gave me at that time could well be applied to other situations, both military and political: 'Lord, give us leaders such that it will be for Your glory to give us victory through them.' "[3]

Derek Prince prayed the news, even though he was in the very center of the news that was happening at that time. Notice how he asked God what he should pray, and then the Holy Spirit led him in a very specific prayer, for which God gave a very specific answer.

As we showed in the previous chapter, God desires that His people partner with Him in prayer to usher in His kingdom in every circumstance, as Derek Prince did in World War II. The Bible speaks of Jesus as "Lord of lords and King of kings" (Rev. 17:14). While God is sovereign, His desire has always been that mankind receives delegated authority on the earth. He has chosen to rule through His people.

The Angel and the Philippines

The Angel of the Lord is going before you—when you leave, it will leave.
PROPHETIC WORD FROM MANILA

If I (Wendy) ever needed divine protection, it was in Zamboanga. My Philippine-based crew and I were flying from Manila to Zamboanga in the southern part of the Philippines to cover the hostage drama of missionaries Martin and Gracia Burnham. It was February 2002, and the notorious Abu Sayyaf, a radical Islamic group, had already held the couple hostage for 10 months. The Abu Sayyaf, with ties to al-Qaeda, was known for two things: kidnapping, especially white tourists, and beheading their victims. A powerful team of believers sent us out from Manila with prayer and this prophetic word: "The Angel of the Lord will go before you, and when you leave, it will leave."

When we landed in Zamboanga, one of the baggage handlers told my Filipino producer Lucille, regarding me, "She's going to be kidnapped." Since he said it in their native Tagalog, I didn't understand. I only knew Lucille was giving him a tongue-lashing for something.

Imagine a tropical paradise, with lush exotic fruits, fresh fish, warm balmy breezes and breathtaking scenery. That is Zamboanga—only wherever we went, we were accompanied by armed gunmen. The fear that permeated the air was thicker than the humidity. It is a land of paradoxes and suspense. On our first night in Zamboanga, Lucille and I had only been asleep for a few minutes when I shot up in bed, shouting, "JESUS, JESUS, JESUS!"

"I feel it too," Lucille screamed.

Something had come into our room. We couldn't see it, but we could sure feel it. I've never felt such a dark and foreboding spirit before. We knelt together on the giant king-sized bed and took authority over the evil spirit, in the name of Jesus. Afterward, even though the lock was broken on our sliding glass door, we lay down and slept like babies. The spirit did not return.

We later felt that it was more than a lower-ranking demonic presence; it may have been a regional principality, perhaps even the spirit of Islam, on a reconnaissance mission to check out the Christian warriors who were invading its territory. Praise God that the name of Jesus is still bigger than any evil. As Jesus said, "I give you the authority to trample on serpents and scorpions, and over all the power of the enemy, and nothing shall by any means hurt you" (Luke 10:19, *NKJV*). Jesus meant what He said.

Dangerous Stand-up

A few days into our trip, we had a chance to go to Basilan Island where the Burnhams were being held hostage. The nature of the journey was dangerous. I had seven armed bodyguards, all with M16 rifles. We took a 45-minute ferryboat ride to the island where we boarded a van and took off into the jungle. I was the only white person in a sea of Filipinos. Even though I was wearing khaki from head to toe, the intense stares from the locals told me that I was definitely not blending in. After some interviews with local police officials, my main goal was to do a stand-up in the jungle, showing where Martin and Gracia had been living all of these months. Although the chances of being ambushed by the Abu Sayyaf were very real, I had a strange sense of peace and literally no fear. After several takes, I felt that we got the stand-up. We got back in the van and started heading back to the dock to catch the ferry. For some reason, our driver began driving dangerously fast, which was much scarier than the jungle stand-up. But somehow, we made it back to the boat and finally back to Zamboanga by nightfall.

Foreign Journalists Off-Limits

Although we had tried to keep a low profile on Basilan Island, the headlines in the newspaper the next day clearly showed us that we had been noticed:

Foreign Journalists Off-Limits to Basilan Island

The newspaper reported that the Abu Sayyaf had made it known that they were looking for more white people, including journalists, to kidnap for ransom; therefore, the police were closing the door to the island. The prophecy we received from Manila had come true: "The Angel of the Lord is going before you, and when you leave, it will leave." Thankfully, in the few short hours we had been there, my crew and I were able to interview and pray with some Filipino women who had been victimized by the Abu Sayyaf. One young lady's brother had been murdered and she herself had been raped. As we prayed for her, we watched as the spirit of God touched her heart and washed away the pain, hate and bitterness.

Her face, which had been so full of pain and torment, broke into a beautiful smile, her eyes full of grateful tears. I realized in that moment that the news story was secondary. We were here for this woman, and Jesus would have sent us halfway around the world just for her—just to tell her how much He loved her, that He hadn't forgotten what happened to her and that He wanted to heal her. What an amazing God we serve who will leave the 99 sheep to go after the 1!

Time to Leave

The next day, as I sat in the hotel's business office, working on my script, the Holy Spirit said, "It's time to leave. It's no longer safe for you to be here." I told my crew we needed to change our tickets and get an earlier flight back to Manila. It was the first time I had felt a sense of uneasiness in my spirit. Peace is always the barometer. When God removed His peace, I knew it was time to go. And God made a way for us to leave early.

Not only did we get the story, but we also prayed for the city's mayor, the police chief, the general of the army and many Abu Sayyaf victims. Unfortunately, four months later, Martin Burnham was shot and killed during a rescue attempt by the Philippine military. Gracia Burnham was shot in the leg, but she survived. She later told me that as harrowing an experience as it was, she wouldn't trade it. "Something very special was going on there when I was held captive. You know, here in the States, if I get thirsty, I go to the sink and get something to drink. And if I get hungry, I go to the fridge and see what's there to munch on. But in the jungle, if I got thirsty, I prayed to God and asked Him for something to drink, and He sent it to me. And it's different now. I got to know Him in a very unique and special way. I guess I wouldn't trade it for anything," she said. And I, too, wouldn't trade my Philippines adventure and how I experienced God there for anything.

Keys to Answered Prayer

Once we know that God desires for us to be intercessors and has given us His authority to co-labor with Him in the Spirit, we need to learn how to pray the news in a way that gets results. The apostle James declared:

The effective prayer of a righteous man can accomplish much (Jas. 5:16).

So how do our prayers become effective? First of all, it is through having a daily intimate relationship with Jesus—by what He called "abiding in the Vine" that we bear much fruit for the Kingdom. Jesus declared:

Abide in Me, and I in you. As the branch cannot bear fruit of itself unless it abides in the vine, so neither can you unless you abide in Me (John 15:4).

Our motivation in prayer will flow from our relationship with Jesus. Our compassion toward others will be birthed from our love for God. Our ministry will then come from the overflow of our relationship with the Lord. Jesus went on to say:

I am the vine, you are the branches; he who abides in Me and I in him, he bears much fruit, for apart from Me you can do nothing. If anyone does not abide in Me, he is thrown away as a branch and dries up (John 15:5-6).

Jesus was making a clear contrast between those who have an intimate relationship with Him who bear much fruit, and those who do not. We need to walk humbly before God, knowing that apart from Him, we can do nothing and our prayers will be ineffectual.

To try to pray and minister apart from an intimate relationship with Jesus is to have a "works-oriented" ministry, which Jesus calls a "dried-up branch." This striving in our own power and effort will bear little eternal fruit. In the end, a works-oriented ministry is spiritual wood, hay and stubble that will burn up in the fire.

But look at the power we receive in prayer when we abide in Jesus.

He promised, "If you abide in Me, and My words abide in you, *ask whatever you wish,* and it will be done for you" (John 15:7, emphasis added).

Our chief priority must be the First Commandment: "You shall love the Lord your God with all your heart, and with all your soul, and with all your mind" (Matt. 22:37). Then from the relationship built in honoring the First Commandment, we can follow through with true fruitfulness in the Second Commandment: "You shall love your neighbor as yourself" (Matt. 22:39).

As we walk in this intimate relationship with God, and as He answers our prayers, our lives become fruitful for the Kingdom. In all of this, God is glorified.

My Father is glorified by this, that you bear much fruit, and
so prove to be My disciples (John 15:8).

As we pray the news in faith, motivated by our love for God and our compassion for others, we will see Him answer that prayer and move mightily. He wants to answer these prayers. In Matthew 6:33, we read that if we "seek first His kingdom and His righteousness" by abiding in Jesus through our love relationship, then "all these things will be added to [us]," and we will bear much fruit.

The Disciplines of Prayer

Jesus tells us in the Great Commission (see Matt. 28:19-20) that we are to go into all the world and make disciples. The root word of disciple is "discipline." Our calling is to go into all the world and make disciplined followers of Jesus. There are spiritual disciplines that are required of the mature Christian—not as law, but as the condition for walking in blessing, anointing and power. While we are saved by grace, and we live by grace, there is a disciplined effort that we need to put forth as co-laborers with God. The apostle James wrote, "Even so faith, if it has no works, is dead, being by itself" (Jas. 2:17).

Our prayer life can be like someone who is baking cookies. If you put dough into a heated oven, after a prescribed time you will have delicious cookies to eat. If, like a child you put mud pies into the oven, you will only receive hot, dried mud in the end. It's the same in our spiritual lives. In many ways we receive from God in proportion to what we give. For "whatever a man sows, that he will also reap" (Gal. 6:7, *NKJV*).

In order to have God's results as we pray the news, we need to intercede in the way that God directs in His Word. So here are some biblical principles that you can employ to make your prayer life more effective and fruitful for the Kingdom.

Pray in Faith

"Prayer," said E. M. Bounds, "projects faith on God, and God on the world. Only God can move mountains, but faith and prayer move God."[4] The only way to be effective in prayer is to ask in faith.

> And Jesus answered saying to them, "Have faith in God. Truly I say to you, whoever says to this mountain, 'Be taken up and cast into the sea,' and does not doubt in his heart, but believes that what he says is going to happen, it will be granted him. Therefore I say to you, all things for which you pray and ask, believe that you have received them, and they will be granted you" (Mark 11:22-24).

Praying in faith is a prerequisite to God's moving on our behalf. The apostle James wrote concerning prayer:

> But he must ask in faith without any doubting, for the one who doubts is like the surf of the sea, driven and tossed by the wind. For that man ought not to expect that he will receive anything from the Lord, being a double-minded man, unstable in all his ways (Jas. 1:6-8).

Faith is the currency of heaven. It is by faith that we receive salvation in the first place (see Eph. 2:8). Everything that God wants to give us in this life is only received through faith. There are two times in the Gospels where we see that Jesus marveled.

One time He was amazed at the unbelief of the people from His hometown:

> Now He could do no mighty work there, except that He laid His hands on a few sick people and healed them. And He *marveled* because of their unbelief (Mark 6:5-6, *NKJV*, emphasis added).

The other time was when the Roman centurion asked him to heal his servant:

> "But say the word, and my servant will be healed. For I also am a man placed under authority, having soldiers under me. And I say to one, 'Go,' and he goes; and to another, 'Come,' and he comes; and to my servant, 'Do this,' and he does it." When Jesus heard these things, He *marveled* at him, and turned around and said to the crowd that followed Him, "I say to you, I have not found such great faith, not even in Israel!" (Luke 7:7-10, *NKJV*, emphasis added).

Faith moves the heart of God. It is vital that we stand in faith as we pray, asking and believing for God to intervene and change the course of world events.

One example of this kind of world-changing prayer comes from a colleague of ours from CBN News, Drew Parkhill. Drew shared how in 1981, he made it a practice to pray for various people every morning, including President Reagan.

"Among other things, I prayed for their protection from the enemy ('warfare prayers' as they are called). One morning, I must have forgotten to pray for the president, or perhaps I was rushed and simply cut my prayers short. Whatever the reason, as I was walking out my bedroom door, I felt like God stopped me and said 'Pray for the president.' So I went back and I did."

As it turned out, that was the day the president was shot. As the world later learned, the president came very close to dying that day. "I'm sure many other believers were led to pray for the president's safety before that attack on his life," Drew explains. "I heard later that a church in Texas had had a word from the Lord to 'break the power of death over President Reagan.' "

Today, even Reagan's former opponents acknowledge the impact he had, not only on America, but also on the world. As Margaret Thatcher said, he won the Cold War without firing a shot. And he restored America's confidence in itself after a decade of scandal, inflation, defeat in Viet Nam, energy shortages, and more.

"We know today what impact Reagan had on the world," Drew notes. "It's hard to imagine how different history might have been had he died on March 30, 1981. But he didn't—because God had other plans, and He made sure they were carried out through prayer."

Fear to Faith

One of the most powerful benefits you will receive as you pray the news is to move from fear to faith. So much of what we see in the media seems ominous, as if the world could come to an end tomorrow. But in praying the news, we choose to keep our eyes on Jesus, who is the author and finisher of our faith (see Heb. 12:2).

Both faith and fear are powerful spiritual forces that can open us up to either blessings from God or attacks from the enemy. As we have already shown, faith moves God to action on behalf of His people. But fear can have the same effect in a negative direction. After calamity struck Job's house, he confessed, "What I feared has come upon me; what I dreaded has happened to me" (Job 3:25, *NIV*). Life and death are both in the power of what we say and in what we believe.

Fear can be overcome by meditating on the promises that God gives to His people in the Bible. Author Candy Arrington shares that her mother was so frightened of what was happening in the world that she wouldn't watch the news. But through prayer and the promises of Scripture, Candy was able to minister hope to her frightened mom.

"My mother worried constantly about finances, taxes, potential home repairs, the health and safety of her loved ones and world events. One day I mentioned something I'd read in the newspaper and another report I'd heard on the evening news. 'I don't read the paper anymore or watch the news,' Mama said. 'I don't even like to answer the phone because I'm afraid it will be bad news.'

"I sat down beside my mom, held her hand, and said, 'You don't have to be afraid of the future. God has taken care of you all these years. He isn't going to abandon you now.' Tears glazed her eyes and her chin quivered. As we held hands, I prayed with her and for her. I asked God to help her trust in His unfailing love and power to protect. Then we looked up several verses that spoke to her anxiety level.

"In the years that followed, Mama seemed calmer about all the issues that were sources of anxiety for her before. 'Tell me the news,' she'd say. If there was something disturbing, she'd reach out her hand to mine and we'd hold hands and pray.

"In going through Mama's things following her death, I looked at the flyleaf of her Bible and I found these words in her handwriting:

> Do not be anxious about anything, but in every situation, by prayer and petition, with thanksgiving, present your requests to God. And the peace of God, which transcends all understanding, will guard your hearts and your minds in Christ Jesus (Phil. 4:6-7, *NIV*).

> Cast all your anxiety on him because he cares for you (1 Pet. 5:7, *NIV*).

"I believe these verses, and prayer, lessened Mama's fears and provided peace in the final years of her life."[5]

Just as Candy ministered peace to her mother through prayer and the promises of God's Word, so too we can overcome any fear that we encounter while watching the news so that we can be God's co-laborers in intercession. And God is pleased with us when we rise up in faith and action for His kingdom purposes.

> But without faith it is impossible to please Him, for he who comes to God must believe that He is, and that He is a rewarder of those who diligently seek Him (Heb. 11:6, *NKJV*).

The apostle James wrote of the power of faith-filled prayer: "The earnest prayer of a righteous person has great power and produces wonderful results" (Jas. 5:16, *NLT*). Then he went on to share the faith-filled example of the prophet Elijah:

> Elijah was as human as we are, and yet when he prayed earnestly that no rain would fall, none fell for three and a half years! Then, when he prayed again, the sky sent down rain and the earth began to yield its crops (Jas. 5:17-18, *NLT*).

As New Testament believers, we can walk in the same power as this great man of God as we follow the leading of the Holy Spirit in faith. Jesus taught His disciples two key truths regarding faith: (1) "With God all things are possible" (Matt. 19:26, *NKJV*), and (2) "All things are possible to him who believes" (Mark 9:23).

It's easier for us to say "with God all things are possible" than to say "all things are possible to him who believes." But we must also realize that Jesus made both of these statements, and they are equally true. As we pray the news, let us seek to please God by praying in faith, believing that as we do, He will respond mightily and change the course of history.

Pray According to God's Word

There is tremendous power in the Word of God, whether spoken, prayed or meditated upon.

> So will My word be which goes forth from My mouth; it will not return to Me empty, without accomplishing what I desire, and without succeeding in the matter for which I sent it (Isa. 55:11).

There is a scene in the movie *Dune*, which is a messianic allegory, where the army has weapons that work in response to spoken commands. At one point the "messiah" character of the movie is approaching one of the warriors whose weapon is turned on.

When the warrior speaks the "messiah's" name, his voice-activated weapon discharges and blows a hole in the side of the mountain. That is how powerful the name of Jesus is in prayer. That is also how powerful the Word of God is when spoken in prayer or declared in faith.

Scripture tells us that life and death are in the tongue (see Prov. 18:21). So when we pray the Scriptures in faith, we are speaking the life of God into the atmosphere. There is tremendous power that goes forth when we pray according to the Word of God.

Author Peter Lundell describes how the Early Church understood the power of praying the Scripture: "In Acts 4:23-31 when the Jewish ruling council released Peter and John from their arrest, the two reported back to the Jerusalem church. Immediately all the people gathered there joined together in a loud group prayer. They started by giving glory to God. Then they prayed Scripture by quoting Psalm 2:1-2. After this they presented to God the problem of the political opposition they faced, and they offered themselves to be part of God's answer. They did not pray for their own protection, only for power to witness and do miracles. God shook the place, apparently with an earthquake, and filled them with the Holy Spirit.

"Praying the Scripture for the Early Church meant that they related a Bible verse to their personal situation. In their case, Psalm 2:1-2 spoke prophetically of earthly rulers who stood against God and particularly against the Messiah—just as the Jewish leaders now stood against them and their proclamation of Jesus the Messiah.

"In the same way, we can apply a Bible verse to whatever we face . . . Even if the outcome is not miraculous, God's Word still gives us comfort, hope and courage to face our challenge. . . . Praying according to biblical promises guides my prayer and increases my faith for an answer. It's as though I'm praying along with God rather than on my own."[6]

"God knows what his Word says," Lundell continues. "He doesn't need us to tell him. So although we give glory to God by praising Him with what's written, we pray His Word mainly for our sakes. Internalizing what the Bible says builds our confidence when we pray, because we're praying not merely by our own desires but according to his promises."[7]

A great champion of prayer in history was Madame Jeanne Guyon, who lived in France at the turn of the eighteenth century. She is known for her teachings on contemplative prayer and intimacy with God. She taught the radical idea for the day that any serious Christian could have an intimate relationship with God. This message of love and liberty delighted the common people, but it threatened the leadership of the Roman Catholic Church, who imprisoned her for years. Madame Guyon was one of the first people to advocate praying the Scripture:

> You do not read quickly; you read very slowly. You do not move from one passage to another, not until you have *sensed* the very heart of what you have read. You may want to take that portion of Scripture that has touched you and turn it into prayer. Praying the Scripture is not judged by *how much* you read but by the *way* you read. If you read quickly, it will benefit you little. You will be like a bee that merely skims the surface of a flower. Instead, in this new way of reading with prayer, you become as the bee who penetrates into the *depths* of the flower.[8]

Lundell teaches that Guyon's approach goes beyond understanding what God's Word means to grasping its intention: "If we grab a handy Bible verse and use it to get what we want, we may be playing games rather than praying Scripture. But when we let a verse penetrate our thinking and apply it to our situation, then address it back to God, that's praying Scripture. We're thinking God's thoughts after him, praying according to His will as recorded for the ages.

"When we pray Scripture, we actually hold God to His Word. That's a scary thought. Who are we to hold the almighty God to His Word? This is who: His children. John 1:12 says that to all who receive and believe Him, He gives the right to become children of God. Hebrews 4:16 tells us we can approach the throne of grace with confidence. Yet few of us experience the fullness of God's promises. . . . He answers and blesses those of us who believe God's Word and claim it in our prayers."[9]

It is the wise intercessor who wields the Sword of the spirit—the Word of God—in prayer.

Walk in Forgiveness

Forgiveness is one of the most powerful forces in the universe. There is freedom in forgiveness. There is healing in forgiveness. There is peace in forgiveness. And there is power in prayer when we forgive.

In the prayer that Jesus taught His disciples, He instructed all believers to pray, "Forgive us our sins, as we have forgiven those who sin against us" (Matt. 6:12, *NLT*). Another time He declared:

> So if you are presenting a sacrifice at the altar in the Temple and you suddenly remember that someone has something against you, leave your sacrifice there at the altar. Go and be reconciled to that person. Then come and offer your sacrifice to God (Matt. 5:23-24, *NLT*).

The Bible tells us, "If it is possible, as far as it depends on you, live at peace with everyone (Rom. 12:18, *NIV*). Of course, forgiveness sounds great. But sometimes it's difficult to actually give to another—especially if we have been badly hurt. But just like in giving love, the giving of forgiveness is, at its core, a decision. It is a matter of obedience to a holy God of love who desires that we love like He does. So it requires grace and faith—just like everything we receive from heaven. But we need to remember that forgiveness is a command of God, not a suggestion:

> Whenever you stand praying, forgive, if you have anything against anyone, so that your Father who is in heaven will also forgive you your transgressions. But if you do not forgive, neither will your Father who is in heaven forgive your transgressions (Mark 11:25-26).

As you prepare to pray the news, if there is anyone you need to forgive, take a moment to do so right now. And if you are having a hard time forgiving that person, ask the Lord to give you His grace to do so. You will be amazed at what God can do with a person who is willing to forgive—even if he or she doesn't feel like it.

Be Persistent in Prayer

In Jesus' teaching on prayer, He shared this parable:

> Then He said to them, "Suppose one of you has a friend, and goes to him at midnight and says to him, 'Friend, lend me three loaves; for a friend of mine has come to me from a journey, and I have nothing to set before him'; and from inside he answers and says, 'Do not bother me; the door has already been shut and my children and I are in bed; I cannot get up and give you anything.' I tell you, even though he will not get up and give him anything because he is his friend, yet because of his persistence he will get up and give him as much as he needs" (Luke 11:5-8).

Then Jesus added this instruction:

> So I say to you, ask, and it will be given to you; seek, and you will find; knock, and it will be opened to you. For everyone who asks, receives; and he who seeks, finds; and to him who knocks, it will be opened (Luke 11:9-10).

Luke uses three key words here that are full of meaning to help us understand the need for persistence in our prayers: "ask," "seek" and "knock." The Greek word for "ask" is αἰτέω, *aiteo,* meaning "to request." The Greek for "seek" is ζητέω, *zeteo,* which means "to seek." And the Greek word for "knock" is κρούω, *krouo,* which means "to strike." But in all three cases, each and every time they are mentioned in this passage, the verses are in the present active tense, which indicates "a processing," or an "undefined" aspect to the actions. In other words, the literal translation of this passage reads, "Keep asking, and it will be given to you; keep seeking, and you will find; keep knocking, and it will be opened to you."

On another occasion, Jesus used another parable to illustrate the vital importance of persistence in our prayers:

> Now He was telling them a parable to show that at all times they ought to pray and not to lose heart, saying, in a certain city there was a judge who did not fear God and did not respect man. There was a widow in that city, and she kept coming to him, saying, "Give me legal protection from my opponent." For a while he was unwilling; but afterward he said to himself, "Even though I do not fear God nor respect man, yet because this widow bothers me, I will give her legal protection, otherwise by continually coming she will wear me out" (Luke 18:1-5).

Then Jesus gave the moral of the story:

> And the Lord said, "Hear what the unrighteous judge said; now, will not God bring about justice for His elect who cry to Him day and night, and will He delay long over them?" (Luke 18:6-7).

As we pray the news, we need to ask and keep on asking, despite what we see with our eyes. Our role is to pray that God's will be done. We do that by praying according to the Scriptures, which we know is God's revealed will. Then we stand in faith until we see His will established and fulfilled in any and every situation.

Be Led by the Spirit in Prayer

We have already shown that as believers, we are joint heirs with Jesus Christ. Paul told the church in Rome that the Spirit of God leads all those who are the children of God (see Rom. 8:14). The context of Romans 8 is living in the Spirit, and not according to the flesh. Life in the Spirit is supposed to be the norm for the New Testament Christian. Scripture tells us that our steps are to be led by the Spirit:

> The steps of a good man are ordered by the LORD, and He delights in his way (Ps. 37:23, *NKJV*).

> Your ears will hear a word behind you, "This is the way, walk in it," whenever you turn to the right or to the left (Isa. 30:21).

God is spirit, and He communicates with us through our spirit. So we must learn to tune our ears to recognize His voice. When the prophet Samuel first heard the voice of God as a young boy, he confused it with the voice of his teacher, Eli. It is often the same with us as we grow in hearing our heavenly Father. Every believer needs to "learn to discern" God's voice for himself/herself. The writer of Hebrews tells us that this discernment comes from practice:

> But solid food belongs to those who are of full age, that is, those who *by reason of use* have their *senses exercised to discern* both good and evil (Heb. 5:14, *NKJV*, emphasis added).

In His earthly ministry, Jesus continually modeled Spirit-led prayer—especially at key moments of decision. When He was preparing to choose from the large group of His followers the men who would be His 12 apostles, the Bible tells us that He first inquired of the Lord in prayer:

> Now it came to pass in those days that He went out to the mountain to pray, and continued all night in prayer to God. And when it was day, He called His disciples to Himself; and from them He chose twelve whom He also named apostles (Luke 6:12-13, *NKJV*).

Jesus taught that He did nothing without inquiring of His Father:

Therefore Jesus answered and was saying to them, "Truly, truly, I say to you, the Son can do nothing of Himself, unless it is something He sees the Father doing; for whatever the Father does, these things the Son also does in like manner" (John 5:19).

God desires that we all follow in the footsteps of Jesus and live a life that is directed by the Spirit. Jesus promised that the Holy Spirit would be our guide in prayer, and in all of life.

But the Helper, the Holy Spirit, whom the Father will send in My name, He will teach you all things, and bring to your remembrance all that I said to you (John 14:26).

But when He, the Spirit of truth, comes, He will guide you into all the truth; for He will not speak on His own initiative, but whatever He hears, He will speak; and He will disclose to you what is to come (John 16:13).

The apostle Paul called on the Ephesians to be led by the Spirit in prayer:

With all prayer and petition pray at all times in the Spirit, and with this in view, be on the alert with all perseverance and petition for all the saints (Eph. 6:18).

It is the Spirit-led believer who is most effective in prayer.

When Colette Branch, who owns an independent living services business for disabled people in New Orleans, heard that a Category 5 storm was approaching, she started to pray, and God told her, "Get out of here. Don't wait. Whatever you have to do, leave." She and everyone who depended on her—nearly 100 severely disabled people and about 200 employees and their families—packed up and left town.

"I told everyone that I would buy Six Flags passes for the clients and for the workers. I said to look on the bright side; if we left and it was unnecessary, we would consider it a vacation. That way, no matter what happened we were safe."

Ten months before Katrina hit, another potential hurricane threatened the area. The mayor of New Orleans issued a voluntary evacuation order. The poorly organized evacuation resulted in solid, wall-to-wall, unmoving traffic. People were stuck on the roads for hours. There were people hospitalized for dehydration and a bus caught on fire, full of elderly people. Colette took the false alarm as God's warning to prepare, whereas others were angry and felt even less willing to consider evacuating when Katrina entered the Gulf in August 2005.

Colette's caravan did not encounter any traffic. Despite all the organization of bringing together such a large group of people, they left New Orleans by midday on Saturday. Most others didn't leave until Saturday night or Sunday morning. We know now that some didn't make it out alive. But because Colette prayed continually and listened to God, she saved hundreds of lives.[10]

The seventeenth-century Quaker leader Isaac Penington wrote of prayer: "You must press your spirit to bow daily before God and wait for breathings to you from his Spirit. . . . By His secret working in your spirit, giving you assistance from time to time, you will advance nearer and nearer towards the kingdom."[11]

This is the Spirit-filled, Spirit-led life that God desires for each of us. Those who will hone sensitivity to the leading of the Spirit in their lives will have tremendous authority as they pray the news.

Pray in Agreement

There is tremendous power when Christians come together to pray in agreement. Jesus declared:

> Again I say to you, that if two of you agree on earth about anything that they may ask, it shall be done for them by My Father who is in heaven. For where two or three have gathered together in My name, I am there in their midst (Matt. 18:19-20).

The psalmist declared, "Behold, how good and how pleasant it is for brothers to dwell together in unity! . . . For there the LORD commanded the blessing—life forever" (Ps. 133:1,3). Unity among believers brings both power in prayer, and also the blessing of God.

Pray in Humility

Prayer helps us to gain an accurate understanding of who we are as finite, mortal human beings in relation to an infinite and immortal God. As we grow in our relationship with God, we increase in our awe and wonder of the Creator of the universe. Humility is a key element in answered prayer. God declares:

> If . . . My people who are called by My name *humble themselves and pray* and seek My face and turn from their wicked ways, then I will hear from heaven, will forgive their sin and will heal their land (2 Chron. 7:13-14, emphasis added).

We see in this verse that humility is a condition that the Lord places on His people in prayer. And our prayer is not to be some sort of public show:

> When you pray, you are not to be like the hypocrites; for they love to stand and pray in the synagogues and on the street corners so that they may be seen by men. Truly I say to you, they have their reward in full. But you, when you pray, go into your inner room, close your door and pray to your Father who is in secret, and your Father who sees what is done in secret will reward you (Matt. 6:5-6).

The apostle James spoke very directly concerning the need for humility:

> Humble yourselves in the presence of the Lord, and He will exalt you (Jas. 4:10).

> God is opposed to the proud, but gives grace to the humble (Jas. 4:6).

The apostle Peter quoted this same proverb from the Old Testament, and then added, "Therefore humble yourselves under the mighty hand of God, that He may exalt you at the proper time" (1 Pet. 5:6).

Show Yourself Approved

There are some who receive the call of God, but then they never do anything tangible or practical to respond to that call. As a result, they never fulfill the call of God in their life. It's like a person who is called to be an overseas missionary who never studies cross-cultural communication and never gets a passport.

The apostle Paul spoke this admonition to Timothy, one of his protégés in the ministry: "Be diligent to present yourself approved to God as a workman who does not need to be ashamed, accurately handling the word of truth" (2 Tim. 2:15).

What we can imply by Paul's statement here is that if one avoids this diligence to study, you can find yourself ashamed for not accurately handling the word of truth. So as we respond to God's calling to pray the news, there are some practical things that we can do to be fully armed and equipped for the battle that will inevitably come:

- Be an active member of a Bible-believing church.
- Establish a healthy relationship with your pastor.
- Find a spiritual mentor—someone who is mature in the Lord and can pray with you and answer questions when needed.
- Be a life-long student of the Bible—never stop learning God's Word.
- Have a prayer room, or find a few good spots where you like to intercede.
- Join a team of intercessors—don't be a lone ranger in prayer, but ask the Lord to help you find others who can be prayer partners.
- Keep a prayer journal—carry it with you to record the things God leads you to pray for, and the answers to those prayers.

- Find a list of intercessory prayer websites where you can learn more about prayer and connect with other intercessors (see our list of recommended websites in the back of the book).
- Keep up to date with prayer resources such as books, e-newsletters and podcasts (see our list of recommended resources).

While it is important to practice these spiritual disciplines, it is also good to know a little bit about the media, about government and about the world of journalism. Here are some practical suggestions to consider as you begin to pray the news:

- If you are not already, become familiar with the political process—know the key positions and the people filling those political posts.
- Create a prayer list of political leaders from all branches of government—federal, state, county and local—then pray through that list on a daily or weekly basis, interceding for the various leaders by name.
- Create a list of key media leaders—reporters, writers, anchors, media owners, opinion makers, TV personalities— and pray for them on a daily or weekly basis.
- Be diligent to keep a media balance—observe a variety of coverage from television, newspapers, magazines, Internet news sites, e-newsletters and radio.
- Read and watch news from the left and the right side of the political spectrum—and from the middle.
- Read and watch news from both secular and Christian sources.
- Read books on understanding culture from a biblical worldview (see our list of recommended reading).
- Consider taking rigorous courses on politics, journalism, leadership or worldview from a Christian media organization or university—an example would be the Charles Colson Center, "Centurions" training program or the Regent University Robertson School of Government.

- Return to college to complete a degree in government, journalism, leadership, media studies or biblical studies with an emphasis on prayer or leadership.
- Subscribe to key blogs or e-newsletters to help you keep up to date on important issues of the day (see our recommended list in the back of the book).
- Get involved in the political process in your community.
- Prayerfully consider running for elected office.
- Volunteer your time, talent and prayer in community service outreach ministry.
- Build relationships and reach out to key influencers on the local, state and national level—these may be leaders in media, government, law, education, business and ministry.

As you step out into this ministry of praying the news, ask the Lord, your spouse, your pastor, mentor and friends to help you keep a spiritual balance, and consider these suggestions:

- Don't let the news or politics become an idol—watch and pray the news, but don't be consumed by it.
- Set a schedule to guard your family time and your other responsibilities.
- If you find the news starting to become overwhelming in any way—or if it is consuming too much of your time and energy, or becoming an idol—back away for a time and focus on abiding in Jesus and worshiping God. Then when you feel a release, slowly ease yourself back into praying the news.
- Be led forth in peace when praying the news (see Isa. 55:12)—if you begin to become angry, fearful or overly frustrated, take a break and seek the Lord. In His presence is fullness of joy (see Ps. 16:11).
- Schedule time away from your ministry to be refreshed with the Lord and with your family. A good rule to follow: divert daily, withdraw weekly, move out monthly, escape annually.

- Recognize that true change doesn't come from government, but from the hand of God.
- Pray without ceasing by the leading of the Holy Spirit—and not only for the events in the news.
- Stand in faith and expect an answer!

Praying the News: Watchmen on the Wall

The prophet Isaiah spoke of those who move in the ministry of intercession as watchmen on the wall.

> O Jerusalem, I have posted watchmen on your walls; they will pray day and night, continually. Take no rest, all you who pray to the LORD. Give the LORD no rest until he completes his work, until he makes Jerusalem the pride of the earth (Isa. 62:6-7, *NLT*).

From your post atop the spiritual wall, you are watching the spirit realm and praying by the leading of the Holy Spirit. In this way, you are like the sons of Issachar: "Of the sons of Issachar, men who understood the times" (1 Chron. 12:32).

Jesus said, "The kingdom of heaven (dominion of the King) suffers violence, and violent men take it by force" (Matt. 11:12). As we contend for the Kingdom in praying the news, we will bind the strong man (see Matt. 12:29) and take by force all that God has prepared for us to accomplish in His will. By praying the news, we enter into this calling to be a "watchman on the wall"—this calling to pray without ceasing that God's kingdom would come on the earth as it is in heaven.

THE CITY OF HOPE

Manchester, Kentucky, nestled in the beautiful and wild Daniel Boone National Forest, was once known as the "pain killer capital of the nation," and drug dealing was actually considered part of the local economy. The drug dealers, who mainly sold methamphetamines and OxyContin, were running the town along with several corrupt politicians. The drug problem had gotten so bad that the younger generation of Clay County was literally dying off.

There was a feeling of hopelessness and despair that was almost tangible.

But something extraordinary was about to happen. Desperation led to desperate prayer. "About eight months before the march, we started praying, just a handful of us, crying out to God," said Pastor Doug Abner of Manchester Community Church. "There was a groundswell, and we began to be motivated by the drug problem in our county. As we began to pray, we felt that God was really speaking to us out of Isaiah 60":

> Arise, shine; for your light has come, and the glory of the LORD has risen upon you. For behold, darkness will cover the earth and deep darkness the peoples; but the LORD will rise upon you and His glory will appear upon you. Nations will come to your light, and kings to the brightness of your rising (Isa. 60:1-3).

Local pastors who used to barely speak to each other began to meet, and denominational walls that had been in place for decades started to crumble as they cried out to God on behalf of their young people and their city. They planned a march against drugs and corruption to send the drug dealers a message.

The March

On that Sunday, Clay county residents awoke to the sound of a hard-driving rain and unseasonably cold temperatures—not what march organizers were hoping for. One politician sneered, "If it rains, there won't be 300 people here."

When Karen Engle, executive director of Operation Unite, an anti-drug task force, asked if the march was still on, Pastor Abner replied, "Drug dealers sell drugs in the rain, young lady; it doesn't slow them down, and it's not slowing us down either."

Still, it was wishful thinking that thousands would leave the comfort of their warm, dry homes to take part in the march. But perhaps many had underestimated the pain and desperation that had gripped the people of this rugged and somewhat isolated community for decades. It was time for a change. It was time to take their streets back from the enemy.

So, despite the rain, they came—not 300, but more than 3,500 people, representing more than 60 churches in Clay County, Kentucky. Men, women and children, many holding colorful banners and posters declaring, "Enough!" gathered near downtown Manchester.

At 3:00 P.M., when the march was set to begin, almost as if on cue, the rain tapered off and so did the chilly gusts of wind as several thousand citizens took off on a somber march through town. Some sang old gospel hymns, while others prayerfully held hands in remembrance of loved ones. Collectively, the citizens sent the drug dealers a message they would never forget: "Get saved or get busted!"

A Holy Moment

In his thick, eastern Kentucky accent, Pastor Abner told the crowd, "This is my home. I don't plan on going nowhere—drug dealers aren't running me off the creek. This is where I live."

In what many believe was the key to the success of that march, the pastors of Clay County from every denomination stopped in the city's park and repented. They asked God to forgive them for being more concerned about their buildings and programs than the kingdom of God and the people of Clay County.

Pastor Wendell Carmack of Island Creek Baptist Church in Manchester stood on the platform and addressed the large crowd with a prayer: "We confess our sin, Father, that we have failed to do the right thing. Lord, as pastors, as churches, as Christians and citizens, we have too long hid our heads in the sand and not stood up to the evil and the poison of drugs in this county and this community."

According to Pastor Abner, the moment the pastors and the people repented, "something in the Spirit broke in Clay County, Manchester, Kentucky, that has changed us forever. God settled in our community, and a holy thing took place. It's just such a holy thing that's happened. You could feel it. We were in the presence of the living God. I had the thought to take my shoes off. It was one of those God moments that changes history. We really believe from that moment until now that God is tabernacling in Manchester, and we're beginning to see the fruit of what He's doing.

"It's like the bad guys, the drug dealers and corrupt folks, they looked in at the church and all of a sudden they saw 3,500 people that had had enough! The fear of the Lord gripped our city, there's no doubt about that."

The Fear of the Lord

After the march, things began to change almost immediately. Drug arrests went up by 300 percent in the first year. Drug dealers started getting saved and coming to church. Corrupt politicians were arrested or voted out of office.

The story of Manchester aired on *The 700 Club*, inspiring other towns with the same problems to hold their own marches. Thousands of people emailed, called or literally showed up at Community Church in Manchester, saying, "This is where I heard I can find hope."

MANCHESTER,
CITY OF HOPE
PHOTO BY JOHN BECKNELL

"We've been told by drug dealers who've now been set free by Jesus that if they were still dealing drugs they wouldn't even stop in our town and buy gas because the climate has changed so much," Abner said. "Now, many of our churches think it's kind of cool to have drug addicts. They make incredible church members once they're converted."

Suddenly, the town that had been hopeless was exuding hope.

The metamorphosis was so great that city leaders decided they needed to reflect what was happening by changing the name of their city (see the photo above).

Transformation

That hope has permeated nearly every facet of society in Manchester. Transformation can be seen everywhere—from the changed drug culture to the cleanup of political corruption. Even the land is coming back to life. That caught the attention of George Otis, Jr., a man who has researched nearly 800 cases of transformation revival around the world. But until he heard about the miracle in Manchester, Otis said he had not found a town in America that fit all the criteria.

"When God comes, He comes like a divine chiropractor," said Otis. "He snaps things back into alignment that have been out of alignment, whether it's in the political sphere, the economic sphere or the ecological sphere.

"In true transformation, the increased presence of God always affects the land," Otis said. "A few years ago, there were no elk in this part of Kentucky. But right now, they have the largest elk population east of the Mississippi. The black bear have also returned in very large numbers, which has brought tourists back into the area. This has begun to rekindle the economy in some of the local communities."

Even the city's water is better. In 2008, Manchester was awarded for having the best-tasting water in Kentucky.

Otis was so impressed with what God had done in Manchester that he produced a two-hour documentary called *Appalachian Dawn*. It tells the story of how God took a region plagued for centuries by corruption and darkness and turned it into a city of hope. Along with local church leaders, Otis took the documentary on a 50-city "Hope for America" tour where countless people around the country were encouraged to seek God for transformation in their own cities.

Pastor Abner says that what's happening in Manchester today was actually prophesied many years ago. "One day, a lady was on the Daniel Boone Parkway, which runs through Manchester, and she came to my bookstore with a word about a dove in the sky. She saw it three times, and it was pointed in different directions, all pointed back to Manchester. 'I've come to tell you that God said

He's going to do a work in this town, that when it's completed no man can take credit for it because it's so big.'"

"Never in our wildest imagination could we ever believe that God would have done what He's done in a poor place like Manchester, Kentucky. But when He settled in this little valley on the day of the march, He literally changed everything."

Tragedy to Triumph Through Prayer

As the people of Manchester, Kentucky, demonstrated, praying the news can change the course of events. This is true on the regional level, but it is equally true in the lives of individuals and families. Becky Spencer was an English teacher at a Christian school who prayed the news with her students. Little did she know how this act of love would not only touch her community, but her own family, as well.

"Normally, I only took prayer requests from my junior high English students during first hour. But on this crisp fall day the requests kept coming. The front page of our local newspaper was the reason. We were all haunted by the forlorn picture of four children whose mother was missing."

The oldest child, Polly, was 12 years old, just like half of Becky's students. "I could tell they had put themselves in her shoes, imagining her fears and wondering if hope could survive under such conditions. Praying for Polly's mom to be found was a lot more pressing than conjugating verbs. Polly's siblings were Jeri, 10; Ashley, 6; and Justin, 3. They were nearly the same age as my own children—Sara, who was also 12, trailed by Nathan, 9, and Benjamin, 6.

"My students weren't the only ones who couldn't quit wondering what we'd do if we were in that kind of nightmare. Eagerness and dread battled for the lead as we listened to the evening news and grabbed the paper each morning, hoping for a break in the case, but knowing that every passing day made it less likely the news would be good."

The community prayed for two weeks while the missing woman's children and their dad, law enforcement officials and people from the community searched for Debbie Willis. "We asked for guidance for the searchers so that she'd be found," Becky remembers. "We prayed for comfort for the fears these children were facing. We dared to ask that she'd be okay when she turned up."

But Debbie was not okay. Her lifeless body was found in the water under a bridge not too far from their home. Her husband was arrested for her murder. People in the town wondered what would happen to the children whose parents had *both* been snatched from their lives. There were no newspaper articles to follow up on them, but Becky continued to pray at school—and at home.

During lunch in the school cafeteria, Becky learned that the grandmother of the Willis children had approached her fellow faculty members, Wayne and Lori Johnson. She had asked if they would be willing to take them in. She and her husband were already raising one of their grandchildren, and they didn't feel they could take on so many more. But they wanted a Christian home for the kids.

So far, the only people willing to help the kids were relatives who only wanted one child each. If someone didn't come forward to take them all, they'd be split up from one another. And they desperately needed each other after their great loss. Wayne and Lori were newlyweds who were teaching at the Christian school and pastoring a small church. Although they were moved by the situation, they didn't feel that God was leading them to adopt this needy sibling group.

"As we discussed it further," Becky says, "I reminded Lori that my husband, Tracy, and I had been praying for a year and a half for God to lead us to the child He wanted us to adopt. I couldn't help but wonder aloud if perhaps we could take the children. We were two weeks into our 10-week foster and adoptive parenting training through Social Services."

That night at home, Becky talked to Tracy about the possibility of taking in the children. "As we shared, it seemed unwise to take on the task. For one thing, we were living in a house plenty big for seven children, but we were only renting it, and it was for sale, with a price way out of our range. We also only had a six-passenger sedan, which obviously couldn't accommodate nine people.

Becky continued, "Although it seemed a small thing, I also hated to cook! We knew that on our budget, we wouldn't be able to take that many people out to eat very often. With my teaching duties, we just couldn't see how we would manage under the additional parenting duties. It made more sense to keep praying for God to lead us to one child, younger than our Benjamin, like the birth order book said, so we weren't overextended. Meanwhile, of course, we would keep praying for the Willis kids."

Yet, the more they talked about the Willis children, the more Becky and Tracy wanted them. They couldn't get the picture of their sweet faces out of their minds. "We finally brought in our three children to see what their reaction would be. After all, they would be called upon to make sacrifices. Big ones. But they were unanimously in favor of the idea. We ended the evening prayerfully determined to seek God for wisdom and His plan for these kids, regardless of who would end up taking them into their home."

The next morning at school, Lori approached Becky to say that the grandma wanted to know what we had decided. "Whoa, too fast! I told her we hadn't decided anything, but that we were praying about it. I was in a daze all day, wondering if God was really behind this crazy idea.

"That night, I asked Tracy if he had any direction from the Lord yet. He asked me to bring him his Bible. He turned to Mark 9:37, which *happened* to be his reading that day: 'Whoever receives one of these little children in My name receives Me; and whoever receives Me, receives not Me but Him who sent Me' (*NKJV*). I grinned and asked Tracy if that was a yes. His reply was that he believed that if these children needed us, we should be willing to parent them."

Of course, Becky and Tracy still had no idea what the legalities would be, or even if they were still needed. Perhaps Social Services already had a plan for the kids. Becky went back to school on Friday morning and told Lori she could inform the Willis children's grandma that if it worked out legally, they were willing to take the children.

"So I made a call to Social Services that morning," Becky said, "and learned they didn't even have the case yet. I explained that if they became involved, we would be willing to take the children.

"On Monday morning, Judge Patty Macke Dick awarded us custody of the children! We had a couple of weeks to make preparations, including getting beds and bedding, a used 12-passenger van and a night of prayer with some friends who understood our great need for God's help.

"We got to meet the children once to break the ice. Then they moved in with us on Saturday, October 26, 1991. To say that our lives were turned upside down doesn't even begin to portray the chaos that ensued! My naïve idea that we'd be like the von Trapp family singers from *The Sound of Music* was quickly put to rest! No matching outfits while we traipsed around the fields, my guitar in hand, while singing 'Do Re Mi.' These children weren't looking for a new mother; they were still grieving for the one they'd lost."

Becky had to say goodbye to her unrealistic perception that between Jesus and her love, they would be one big happy family. They were meshing two completely different cultures, even though they were all from the USA. The needs of the new children ran deeper than they would have dreamed.

Becky explains it this way: "Old abuses, fears, distrust, grief, anger—suffice it to say we were in way over our heads. But we survived. We kept the children together. We learned to love each other. We got through many difficult days. And we were all stretched beyond our natural abilities. We learned how much we needed God's Holy Spirit to help us through every day—because each one presented new challenges.

"We found that He was faithful and more than enough. And we learned that was true even when the outcome wasn't what we had hoped for. In fact, we're watching the papers again. Our precious Ashley was in the news. Her boyfriend tried to kill her and he's in jail awaiting sentencing.

"So we're praying the news once again—praying that she will escape the kind of lifestyle and choices that brought her mother to an untimely end; praying that she will find her peace and hope and joy in the Lord; praying that the things she learned in our home will make an eternal difference in her life as she makes changes and a fresh start."

Becky and Tracy continue to pray the news for their community and beyond. "We know that news reports are only a glimpse of the battles going on behind the scenes between Light and darkness. That's why we pray. Our God is on the throne, the History Maker who is never surprised by the headlines. Instead, He's looking for willing hearts to respond in obedience to Him so that His plans—His Good News—can be taken to a hurting world.

"And who knows? As we move past merely being informed about what's happening in the world around us, our prayers could lead us into His assignment for us. It might not ever make international news. But it would be recorded where angels rejoice when good triumphs over evil."[1]

A Battle for Peace

As with Becky and Tracy, sometimes the news can come right into our own homes. In March 2003, as millions of people prayed, America stood poised on the brink of war in Iraq. But for Julie Gillies, whose son, Jason, was in the Army preparing to invade, the intercession was not merely for the nation or for the soldiers, it was for her own family.

As the first images of the invasion flashed across her TV screen, Julie stood in the middle of her family room, tears welling in her eyes. Transfixed, she watched with the rest of the country as history unfolded on live television. The U.S. Army's Third Infantry Division was among the first of the troops to advance into Baghdad. Her firstborn son rolled with them. As Jason prepared for combat, Julie engaged in a battle of her own.

"Jason enlisted with the U.S. Army shortly after the September 11 attacks," Julie says. "His dad and I proudly sported a 'My Son Is Serving in the U.S. Army' bumper sticker on our car. Yet a deep concern nagged my mind, and wishful thinking pestered me. 'Why can't our son just sell life insurance for a living?' I moaned."

Now Jason was somewhere in the Iraqi desert, on the verge of war. At the time, rumors were flying, claiming that Saddam Hussein had nuclear weapons. Julie literally became ill with fear, knowing that if the enemy dropped a single nuclear bomb the entire Third Division would be wiped out, and she would never see her boy again.

"I've always thought of myself as a praying woman who trusts God," Julie explains. "Yet I became engulfed in a gut-wrenching assault on the trust I claimed to possess. My faith stretched as I struggled to maintain hope that our son would be all right. I truly wanted to believe that God would protect him. Though I prayed constantly, I've never felt more helpless. In the midst of a mother's nightmare, I felt betrayed by my own heart and body. I quoted Psalm 56:3 to myself regularly: 'When I am afraid, I will put my trust in You.' In reality, I qualified for much worse than merely afraid. I was flat-out, wobbly-kneed terrified."

Thankfully, the Lord sent reinforcements. That Sunday at church, Julie's pastor announced a time of special prayer for all the families with members currently serving in the military.

"My husband and I came forward with just one other family. We took turns announcing the current location of our sons. When the microphone came to me, I barely choked out the words, 'Our son, Jason, is 50 miles south of Baghdad.' A gasp rippled through the congregation. Those nine words echoed in the sanctuary and reverberated within my soul. After the corporate prayer, I gratefully took my seat. Yet the knots in my stomach stubbornly refused to leave."

Instead of feeling better after being prayed for, Julie's emotions spiraled downward. Necessary bodily needs like eating and sleeping became difficult, if not impossible. Guilt stung her heart when she indulged in a family meal or settled down into a comfortable bed at night. "It just felt plain wrong to enjoy *anything*, knowing that our son faced life or death situations on a daily basis. I tried in vain not to imagine the worst."

As the invasion continued, more distressing rumors circulated. The soldiers' MREs (Meals Ready to Eat) and their rations of other supplies could not keep up with demand. In addition, the news constantly displayed footage of a raging sandstorm that assaulted the troops for several days. Reports even claimed that the soldiers' toilet paper supply disappeared completely. Julie's stress level kicked up several notches. At this rate, she would collapse before the war ended.

"I frantically wondered why I couldn't sense the Lord's presence in the midst of this turmoil," Julie remembers. "Why was I having such a hard time trusting Him?"

On the evening of the tenth day of Operation Iraqi Freedom, Julie's husband, Keith, and their son, Joshua, left to run errands. She stayed home with their daughter, Emily, and began to tidy up after dinner. "As I stood in front of the kitchen sink, I literally felt that I could not go on. Ten days without much sleep or food will do that to a person. Clearly, I had transformed into a stressed-out basket case. Something eventually had to give.

"I grew increasingly desperate to know that our son was going to be all right. I physically craved peace. Somehow, I needed to radically trust God and find peace in the midst of this storm. A Scripture flashed into my mind, and I realized that I needed to put on 'a garment of praise instead of a spirit of despair' (Isa. 61:3, *NIV*). But could I immerse myself in praise at a time like this?"

Praise: A Secret Weapon

Like the desperate woman reaching out to touch the hem of Jesus' garment, Julie grew determined to press past her circumstance and touch the Lord. She knew that God alone possessed the ability to grant her the peace she so desperately desired.

She says, "Wiping my hands on a dishtowel, I slung it over my shoulder and headed into our family room toward the stereo. I turned on a praise and worship CD and cranked up the volume. Soon, that red-checkered dishtowel became airborne. I started swinging it around, singing and dancing throughout the family room. If dancing around my house with a dishtowel was what it took, then so be it.

"Seeing my example, Emily raced into the kitchen and got a dish towel of her own. Together, the two of us sang and danced and praised God, waving our colorful dishtowel banners all over the place. Before I knew it, God's presence absolutely flooded the room. Suddenly, joy and laughter erupted out of me. I was astonished. *I wave dishtowels and God shows up?* My surprise swiftly turned to gratefulness. After 10 miserable, dread-filled days, I literally began to live out the Scripture 'I am overcome with joy because of your unfailing love, for you have seen my troubles, and you care about the anguish of my soul' (Ps. 31:7, *NLT*).

"I perceived the Lord's reassurance as He mercifully placed His promise deep within my heart. At that precise moment, God assured me that He controlled our son's destiny. Overwhelming peace washed over me, completely displacing anxiety and fear. The struggle to trust God disappeared entirely, and I joyfully surrendered Jason into the Lord's capable, loving hands."

Julie's dishtowel worship experience turned out to be a major breakthrough. From that point on, her appetite immediately returned to normal. She also slept remarkably well. And she never again—not even once—worried about her son during the rest of his lengthy time in Iraq.

"Throughout the 15 months that Jason spent 'over there,' I drew near to God and He drew near to me (see Jas. 4:8). As I continued to make time in worship and prayer a priority, God faithfully sustained me."

Julie's family celebrated when Jason finally returned home from Iraq later that summer. She learned that on the very first day of the war, he broke his left arm as he rode in one of the tanks. Unable to stop for medical help, and in spite of the pain, her left-handed son managed to get through those harrowing first few weeks of the war.

"In the end, God answered our prayers and brought our soldier home safely. And this grateful mom learned the priceless value of God's peace in the midst of the battle."[2]

There will be times as we are praying the news that we will be swept up in the emotion of the moment, or into spiritual warfare; or like Julie, into a story that hits close to home. Fortunately, Scripture gives us the template for Christians as we move out in obedience to the Lord in intercession:

Rejoice in the Lord always; again I will say, rejoice! Let your gentle spirit be known to all men. The Lord is near.

Be anxious for nothing, but in everything by prayer and supplication with thanksgiving let your requests be made known to God. And the peace of God, which surpasses all comprehension, will guard your hearts and your minds in Christ Jesus.

Finally, brethren, whatever is true, whatever is honorable, whatever is right, whatever is pure, whatever is lovely, whatever is of good repute, if there is any excellence and if anything worthy of praise, dwell on these things.

The things you have learned and received and heard and seen in me, practice these things, and the God of peace will be with you (Phil. 4:4-9).

PRAYER FOR BELIEVERS IN THE NEWS BUSINESS

Having spent 10 years in secular television before coming to CBN, I (Wendy) am sometimes asked, what's the difference between working in a secular newsroom and working in a Christian newsroom? Well, there are many similarities—but the biggest difference is prayer!

Even as you enter the studio headquarters building at CBN, you notice the Scripture on the wall:

> This gospel of the kingdom will be preached in all the world as a witness to all the nations (Matt. 24:14, *NKJV*).

This is your first clue that this is not a secular organization. Our mission at CBN is truly to reach the world with the gospel of Jesus Christ; and we believe that we are doing that through our various TV shows, humanitarian efforts, Internet discipleship, evangelism outreaches, and more—including the news. It's very exciting to be a part of this dynamic ministry.

Another clue that you've left the secular world is that we have chapel every day at noon. We get paid to take a break, sing, worship and hear someone share from the Word of God. It's a very refreshing part of the day.

But the biggest difference is prayer! We pray before each and every show and in nearly every meeting. I cannot remember not praying before a newscast in more than 12 years at CBN. Sometimes we pray for the people who are in the news, people who are suffering, our troops, or persecuted Christians. But our main purpose is to ask for God's blessing on what we're about to do. We confess our utter dependence on Him. We pray for God to anoint us, strengthen us and give us a spirit of excellence so that He may be glorified through our efforts. We also often pray for souls to come into the Kingdom, even through our newscast.

We Were Created to Pray

Having been in television before I was walking with the Lord, I can tell you, there is no comparison. My first week at CBN, I would cry from pure joy that I was not only allowed but expected to pray at work with my colleagues. It was and still is a little slice of heaven on earth and a relief that it's not about me anymore.

When I first started in the business, it was all about me and climbing the broadcast ladder as fast as I could. Now, it's about using the talents and gifts God has given me in a field that I love so that He might become the famous one.

Praying with Bill O'Reilly

Sometimes I forget what a shock prayer can be for some folks who are not used to it—especially in the workplace. I was in New York a couple of years ago to interview Bill O'Reilly, who had just released a new book. I was sitting on the set of *The O'Reilly Factor* and I asked, "Bill, is it okay if we pray before we get started?"

He gave me a very surprised, and somewhat amused, look and replied, "Are you going to pray that you ask the right questions, or that I give the right answers?" We laughed and I said, "A little of both." He told me that in his 30-plus years of broadcasting, this was a first. Imagine that. No one had ever prayed with Bill O'Reilly before an interview in his entire broadcasting career. But it was so second nature to me, I couldn't imagine not praying. So I felt totally comfortable asking. So, I bowed my head and thanked God for the opportunity to be with Bill, for the platform that God had given him and a few other things that I can't recall because I was a bit star-struck.

But what was really amazing to me was how prayer changed the atmosphere in the studio. When Bill arrived on the set, he had seemed a bit stressed and in a hurry to get the interview over so he could prepare for his evening show. But at the mention of prayer, his whole demeanor changed; he looked at me for the first time, I mean, really looked at me. His face softened and he seemed to thoroughly enjoy himself. In fact, he gave us more time than we were supposed to get with him.

Praying with Ben Stein

I have a similar story with actor, comedian and economist Ben Stein. He was with me in Virginia Beach on the set of our daily afternoon show, *Newswatch*. He was promoting his new documentary *Expelled, No Intelligence Allowed* about how the mainstream science establishment suppresses academics who believe they see intelligent design in nature and who criticize evidence supporting Darwinian evolution.

I knew that Stein was Jewish, and I was a little hesitant to ask, but my zeal took over and I asked him if we could pray before we rolled on the interview. He said that would be fine. I don't remember the prayer so much as his reaction. After I said, "Amen," Stein's face was beaming and he said, "This is going to be the greatest interview I have ever done." And he wasn't joking. He really meant it. I think he really felt something—that "something" being the Holy Spirit, and his countenance reflected it.

We went on to have a very good interview despite the fact that I was laughing through most of it—Ben is very funny. Then, to my surprise, his publicist came up to me and thanked me for the prayer. Although we had not prayed for her specifically, she said, "I was so stressed out before you prayed, and afterwards I felt so much peace." Wow! Prayer is powerful and perhaps even more powerful to those who don't experience it every day.

Another story of prayer left me almost speechless.

I was getting ready to interview another Jewish man, Michael Freund. Freund is founder and chairman of Shavei Israel, an organization that helps Jewish people from all parts of the world return to Israel.

Before we did the interview, I prayed for him and his organization and for Israel. I didn't know at the time that Mr. Freund also writes a syndicated column for the *Jerusalem Post*, called "Fundamentally Freund." So, a couple of weeks later, he sent me an article he had written about his visit to Virginia Beach and CBN, where "the people really love Israel and the Jewish people." He went on to say, "Prior to interviewing me about events in the Middle East for CBN's daily news program, anchorwoman Wendy Griffith did something I never saw a journalist do before. She folded her hands together, bowed her head in prayer and humbly offered a solemn plea: 'Bless Your people Israel and keep them safe,' she said. Peering from behind a video camera, one of the cameramen in the studio then quoted verses from Isaiah about the return of the Jewish people to Zion. 'I pray about this on a daily basis,' he said in earnest."

The article continued, "Where else can one find such a deeply rooted love and concern for God's chosen people? Of course, the fact that many U.S. Christians support Israel is nothing new. Much has been written in recent years about the closer ties that have been forged between the two—a fact that has generated no small amount of controversy among certain more liberal sectors of U.S. Jewry. But after my visit to CBN, and based on previous encounters I have had with the pro-Israel evangelical Christians, I am more convinced than ever that the Jewish state needs to undertake a coordinated effort to nurture and broaden this special relationship.

"The fact of the matter is that Bible-believing Christians, even more so than U.S. Jews, may represent the best hope for ensuring that long-term American support for Israel remains strong."

I love how God took my simple prayer for Israel and moved on this Jewish man's heart to share it with his readers in the *Jerusalem Post*.

Prayer Connections

More than just prayer before an interview, I believe that Bill O'Reilly, Ben Stein and Michael Freund all experienced the love of God through prayer. Someone took the time to lift up their names before the Creator of the universe, and they were visibly moved. I believe it touched them because we are all created to pray. As human beings, we are designed to eat, sleep and work; but more than anything, God designed us to desire communion and friendship with Him—and that is what prayer is. Our spirits long for prayer. Prayer is simply communing with our heavenly Father, and it is born out of a love relationship. If anything less is motivating your prayer life, it won't be as effective, and it probably won't last.

Praying for Believers in the News Room

"You can't say that because the Internet and cable TV have arisen that's why mainstream media has dropped," former news director Jim DeSantis observed as we discussed the current state of journalism. "It's dropped because there's no integrity. The latest polls show that journalists are at the bottom of the pile. They are down there with used car salesmen and politicians. What a tragedy."

According to the "State of the News Media," the annual report on American viewing trends by Journalism.org, "Network news audiences in 2009 . . . continued their long decline. . . . Viewership [for the evening news] fell 2.5% . . . (or 565,000 viewers), but that is about half the number of viewers on average lost annually in the evening over the last two decades."[1] The same decline can be seen in newspaper and magazine news consumption.

While network and print news continues to decline in viewership, cable and Internet news is growing rapidly. But as DeSantis points out, character and truth in media is a major issue that affects those who work in the news media, but more importantly, the audience that views the news. Integrity in the field of journalism is only one of the many things that can be the focus of intercession for those called to pray the news.

The journalism profession is a unique line of work, with unique ethical and professional issues and pressures. In order to pray effectively for those in the news business, one needs a thorough understanding of the issues that reporters, editors, anchors and management face every day.

Newsroom Prayer Matters

"It's funny," veteran journalist Scott Baker said, laughing. "When I got the invitation to talk to you about this, I thought, *This may be the first time anyone has written about this—prayer in the newsroom.*"

Scott worked for years in television news before making a successful transition into Internet journalism. He is now the senior editor of Glenn Beck's news website, TheBlaze.com.

"It is very unusual to work in a media company where prayer is actually a normal thing," Scott said. "Now I work with a company of people who are out to dinner, and it begins with prayer. Some of us were at Glenn Beck's house for a business meeting, and the meeting began with prayer. That's not typical in most media companies."

There are Christian journalists across the country who pray at work on a daily basis, but few are able to do so openly. Veteran television journalist Carolyn Castleberry was the anchor for the 5 o'clock news on WAVY-TV, an NBC affiliate in Hampton Roads, Virginia. She co-anchored with another Christian woman, Alveta Ewell. Carolyn said, "She [Alveta] is the one who encouraged me to pray before each newscast. So, together we would bow our heads and say, 'to Your Glory.' That's it, but it's amazing what those prayers did. We became the number-one newscast, overcoming the huge Oprah lead-in on another channel.

"That was God, not us!" Carolyn exclaims. "Plus, as women in a very competitive business, we became great friends. That was a testimony to the other women at the station."

Early in 2004, local newspaper reporter Deb Wuethrich learned that her column won a 2003 Amy Award of Outstanding Merit from the Amy Foundation, a group whose call is to print biblical truth reinforced with Scripture in secular, nonreligious publications. It was through this honor that she learned of the group's founders, W. James Russell and his wife, Phyllis. In addition to their role of encouraging journalists, Russell had an idea that people who pray for one another in their everyday lives can "disciple a nation."

"I read some materials Russell had compiled under the same title encouraging people to pray not only for their own families, but for their neighbors while engaged in daily pursuits," Wuethrich remembers. "As a small-town reporter, I started taking this to heart, even as I worked my news beats.

"When I was on the police beat, before I tackled a stack of accident and complaint reports each week, I felt God's call to pause a moment, and with Russell's words in mind, I'd pray for those whose names I would encounter, and not just for victims of the crimes. I'd also ask God to guide and teach the perpetrators His will in their situations and turn their hearts toward Him. I'd pray for sound judgment and protection for the officers as well.

"When I encountered long waits in county courtrooms until the case I was there for came before the judges, I'd pray for the people in the room—adjudicators, attorneys, victims, families and those in the jumpsuits facing their bad choices."

Once while watching and praying, Deb observed a young man clad in orange glaring at the young woman who had just testified against him. As she returned to her seat, the man sat at his attorney's table and periodically spun his chair around to glare some more. She felt sorry for the girl and prayed for her. "I wasn't the only one who noticed the exchange," Deb said. "Pretty soon, a female state police officer quietly slid across her front row bench. The next time the young man spun his chair around for the glare, the officer's body shielded the young lady, and boy, was he surprised!

"My thoughts upon seeing this interaction went to how Satan can try to intimidate in a similar fashion, but Jesus Christ shielded us with His own body—and we can claim His power and authority through faith.

"I also pray regularly for the people I meet through my daily work in news gathering, from the baby who lost a leg and both kidneys to disease and needs a transplant, to the trustees who govern our community. People tell me that they pray for these people, too, after reading the stories. It's what the late Mr. Russell had in mind, I think, in encouraging us to pray for each other. I find it gives me peace to have the privilege of bringing people and their situations before God, especially when the job frequently exposes me to those in trouble.

"Sometimes I wonder if my small prayers make a difference, but only God knows the true impact His response may have on another life. Sometimes I think big thoughts with big dreams, such as my desire to write and publish books and maybe become known around the world. And sometimes God quietly reminds me that, at least for the time being, He needs a reporter with a Christian worldview, one who's willing to pray for others, right here in Tecumseh, Michigan."[2]

Prayer in Crisis

"I have vivid memories of prayers during 9-11," Scott Baker recalls. "That whole week spoke to me not only because of the tragedy in the country, but my friend and roommate, Mike Gerson, was a speech writer at the White House. He was busy writing the remarks the president would give at the National Cathedral on the Friday after 9-11. I remember just trying to spend a great deal of that week in prayer. I was wrapped up in the feeling that how the country responded and how our perspective of state would change that week would be important for a generation."

Baker also remembers praying fervently during the collapse of the Quecreek Mine in Western Pennsylvania, in July 2002, where nine miners were trapped underground for several days. "I certainly remember offering prayers of protection and hope for those men in the midst of fear and foreboding that it would end terribly. I worked 16 hours that day and went on the air in the 11 P.M. hour. There was an AP bulletin, and then another co-anchor who was at the scene said, 'You can go with this. They're all alive.' I handed the note to my co-anchor in the studio. She had been an iconic presence in the community for decades, and she just choked up and couldn't speak. I remember saying, 'All nine alive.' "

"I still have people tell me, 'I remember watching you that night, and that was amazing.' I think there was such a cumulative sense of thanksgiving and God's provision that night."

Praying for Truth

"One of the main challenges for a journalist is to get the story right and get it on time," says CBN News Jerusalem Bureau Chief, Chris Mitchell. "Often, journalists are working on a deadline. I think people can and should pray that they report the truth given the pressures they're under.

"Intercede for them to have a passion for the truth. Pray for them to speak, report, broadcast the truth in love. Pray for reporters to overcome their own biases—we all have them.

"Pray for the courage to report truth even when it can be dangerous. Sometimes it can be physical danger or threats.

"We are all bombarded with information these days," Mitchell adds. "For journalists it's even more true since we try and keep up with news as a lifestyle. It's often like trying to get a drink out of a fire hydrant. Pray that they see clearly through the information smog."[3]

Carolyn Castleberry states, "I always prayed and believed firmly that the truth would win. If you present each side with respect and with truth, I believe that God's truth will always win.

"I did a series on abortion, and you absolutely have to present both the pro-life and pro-choice sides. You go into tough situations like that and you can speak to people that you don't necessarily agree with, but if you respect them, and listen to them, and you're fair, people notice. So I would pray that the truth would win out, especially in these difficult situations."

How to Pray for People in Journalism

So how would journalists recommend that we pray for people in the news business?

Joseph Farah says, "One of the things that encourages me in my current role as editor and chief executive officer of WorldNet Daily.com are the comments I receive on a daily basis from readers and visitors who tell me they are praying for me and my company. I've heard some very compelling and credible stories about prayer groups and prayer chains invoking the Holy Spirit for protection around me and WND.com. I've met many earnest people who tell me they have my back in prayer in a very real way.

"I believe it, because I have seen the miraculous results of this intercession over and over again throughout my company's 14 years of existence.

"In a very real way, WND.com was an answer to prayer for me," he explains. "I was not the kind of Christian who was willing to compromise the truth or my faith in any way throughout my daily newspaper career. Of course, that cost me jobs. But I also recognized there were not that many daily newspaper opportunities for a faithful Christian editor or publisher.

"When I left my post as editor in chief of the *Sacramento Union* in 1992, I did not expect to find another comparable-size daily to lead. So, I prayed. Since newspapers were the only thing I had ever trained to do, I just wasn't sure what God had in store for me. But when He gave me the idea for WorldNetDaily.com, I realized this was the thing I had been in training for all my life. This was a chance to reach a worldwide audience of English-speaking people—and maybe, eventually, people of all languages."

Farah points out that the ride has certainly not been without bumps. On several occasions, especially in the early years, Farah and his team faced crises that seemed insurmountable. "On one particular day, I recall coming home to tell my wife, Elizabeth, that I just didn't know how we could keep the doors open the next day. We didn't have any answers—and no earthly hope. So we prayed. The next day the answer presented itself. We've seen that experience repeat itself dramatically several times throughout our company's history.

"I know it wasn't just my prayers, but the prayers of people all over the world that sustained our work."[4]

Mark Martin, an anchor and reporter with CBN News, says, "As a journalist, I would ask people to plead the blood of Jesus over my spirit, mind, emotions and body. We are bombarded with constant negativity. Many of our stories deal with tragedy, sin and fear—stories about disasters, crime, sex trafficking, hideous behavior and a shaky economy. As journalists, I believe we are on the front lines of ministry. We report on situations where the enemy has wreaked havoc, or where people are upholding evil ideologies. Many times we are reporting in a dangerous place.

"We are vessels of God's truth and gatekeepers at the same time, exposing lies and letting through information not found on other mainstream networks. I would ask people to pray that we have the mind of Christ and that we do not succumb to worldly thinking or subtle 'spin.' I would also request that people pray for God's protection and favor and pray against fear and anxiety."[5]

"I had people praying for me for a series I did on miracles," Carolyn Castleberry remembers. "There was one story where a little boy died at a local children's hospital. He was pronounced dead, and there was no heartbeat. But the family had a prayer group interceding. They didn't stop praying, even when the hospital staff said, 'Your son has passed on. You can stop.'

"They kept on praying, and God brought this boy back to life. He was fine. There were no disabilities of any kind, and he was able to go finish school. What was really neat was that the doctors testified to this in my report. They said, 'We can't explain it, but we see this stuff all the time.'

"So when I worked on these stories, I just prayed that God would get the glory."

Pray to Be a Witness

Castleberry also encourages intercessors to pray that the Lord will empower news reporters to live clean, Christlike lives in the midst of the daily chaos of a newsroom. "Pray that they will be an example for Christ. One of the simplest things, and it sounds so absurd to people in the Christian world, is that in the newsroom you have to keep your language clean. Seriously, people used to tell me that the thing that separated me the most was my language. I don't curse. I know that seems like a small thing, but when you're in an environment where f-bombs are being dropped on a daily basis, *how* we live and speak is the biggest testimony we have.

"People are constantly watching and listening to see if our walk matches our talk, in any business. It's hard not to let your language go in the newsroom, because things are stressful. Things are crashing and burning all the time. Live shots are going down and everybody is cursing. But you've got to stay cool.

"I was doing a live shot in Washington, DC, and there was a reporter who was standing behind me trying to make me mess up. It's hard enough to think and speak and do live television all at the same time, but this guy was behind me trying to mess me up. As a believer, you try not to get angry. You try to live the way Christ would live.

"In one place I worked, we had a news director who was actually a great guy, but he had a temper on him. He would come out during the break when things were crashing and burning, or we made a mistake, or a live shot wasn't there and he would yell, "What the *@!?* are you guys doing?" And then they would count us back into the show, 5, 4, 3, 2 . . . and you're supposed to smile and keep your cool and composure when somebody has just been cursing at you.

"Being a Christian sometimes in those situations is very difficult because it's easy to lose your top. But the biggest thing that people noticed was different about me was my language.

"So, pray that the Christians in the field of journalism would be able to exercise one of the fruits of the Spirit, which is self-control. And that goes for other things, like how you live. Are you kind to people?"

Pray for Integrity in Journalism

"If you have an axe to grind, you shouldn't go into journalism. If it is just you getting up there and pounding the pulpit, saying, 'Here's the truth, and here's how I see it, and you'd better see it my way,' then you're probably not going to last very long.

"Glenn Beck says all the time, 'The truth has no agenda.' There is a saying that is written on the Science Building at Wheaton College: 'All truth is God's truth.' If the truth is the truth, then it doesn't need you to spin it. It just needs you to tell it.

"The truth kind of has traction. As we pray for journalists," Scott Baker advises, "it's for that sense they have—that insight—to recognize the truth and separate that from the spin.

"The danger for Christians in journalism is how do you avoid cynicism? How do you preserve your sense of ideals? If you are going to work in a newsroom, you're going to have to develop some very thick calluses to do it. That is what I learned from Morton Blackwell in politics. He said the key to coming to Washington is to not be sucked in by the cynicism, and to hold on to your principles and ideals. And I think that is true for those who are in journalism.

"Someone once said that the problem in this country is not bias in the media, it's laziness in the media," Baker explains. "Everybody tries to find the easiest way to get something done. The pressures to meet the deadlines are high. Journalism models right now are changing like crazy. And journalists are just trying to get their jobs done. So there needs to be prayer for understanding among journalists."

The Need for Christians in Journalism

One of the unintended consequences of the holiness movement within Christianity in the nineteenth and early twentieth centuries was that evangelical Christians as a whole chose to steer clear of careers in the media and the arts. Where once Christians dominated the arts, believers stayed away from the "worldly" media during the critical years when movies, radio and television were invented.

The teaching that predominated Christianity in the Victorian era was, "Wherefore come out from among them, and be ye separate, saith the Lord, and touch not the unclean thing" (2 Cor. 6:17, *KJV*). Any truth taken to an extreme can become error; and sadly, this is what took place in the Church as the electronic media burst upon the world stage. In many ways, Christians have been constantly playing catch-up with the world when it comes to media and the arts.

Things have gotten better for Christians entering media fields in the last 30 years. But one field believers have not embraced in large numbers, sadly, has been journalism. Scott Baker has worked diligently to reverse this trend. For years he has encouraged young people through his seminars at Morton Blackwell's Leadership Institute in Washington, DC.

Baker says, "As I've talked about content problems in the media, often evangelicals may feel disrespected by the mainstream media. They tend to focus a good deal of antagonism on the media reporters. I have said in large part that there is a very clear process of blame here. And I place it upon the conservatives. They didn't do those jobs for generations."

After Scott graduated from Wheaton College, he did a fellowship in New York City with the International Radio and Television Society, which placed him as a field producer at CBS News. A fellow Wheaton grad worked in the sales department at CBS. One day Scott asked her, "Where are the other Christians in the New York media?"

"I don't know any," she said.

Scott was floored. "You're kidding me."

"No, I really haven't met anybody that is an evangelical." She explained that there are many people who have a religious background, but there are few Bible-believing evangelicals. "There was not a conservative evangelical interest in going into mainstream media," Baker explains. "Certainly there was nobody when I was in high school or college that was lifted up as a role model. If you were good at communications, they wanted you to go to church and be a preacher.

"If you were a conservative, you wanted to be a propagandist in the good sense of that word. You wanted to be either a columnist or a talk show host. I still think that college students believe they have some sort of constitutional right to be a columnist or some opinionated blogger. I tried to say you can't be mad that the media is made up of people who don't understand you if you're not willing to be part of that group.

"I had 4,000 students go through the seminar I did at the Leadership Institute for 15 years. My advice to them was, you may get to the place where you're the next Rush Limbaugh, but I want you to tell me a story. I want you to go and dig some facts out. I'd bring in Cal Thomas and Robert Novak and Fred Barnes, and I'd say, "Don't tell these kids about what you do now. Tell them about what you did for decades before you were a commentator.""

Scott gets frustrated with Christians who complain about an anti-Christian bias but do nothing to change the atmosphere in the newsrooms. "I say, 'Yeah, but you're not out there doing the job. It's not that they won't let you.' I have never found any bias or resistance to my presence in the newsroom. So I encouraged people in that direction. But what I found was, not only were conservatives not willing to go and do these jobs, they were highly antagonistic toward the people doing them."

Carolyn Castleberry agrees, and calls for the Church to rise up in intercession for people in the field of journalism. "Pray that the Lord of the harvest would send more workers. If you are a Christian, consider going straight into the trenches—secular news. The Lord will protect and guide you. He has always given me Christian friends, and that makes all the difference.

"At one station, there was a young Christian man who would do tag-team evangelism with me. I'm a better opener. I can go to anybody and get him or her to talk to me. But sometimes I'm a little gun-shy about saying, 'Okay, would you like to bow your head right now and receive Christ?' As a reporter, you talk to some big stars and then lots of regular people, and I would just talk to them in the greenroom and tell them a little bit about my life. So church might come up, or what I was doing that weekend, and I could get people to talk. But then this Christian co-worker would come in while I was getting ready for the news and he would 'close the deal'—he had no qualms about going up to a stranger and asking, 'Do you know Jesus as your Lord and Savior? Would you like to pray right now?'

"And it was amazing how many people said, 'Yes.'

"Wherever I've been, God has divinely placed Christian friends in my life," Castleberry explains. "So pray that the Lord of the harvest would send more workers into the field of journalism, because that made all the difference everywhere I was."

Pray for the Management

"I think you have to pray for the corporate side of things," former news director Jim DeSantis explains. "Pray that God puts people in place that can make a difference."

"Pray for the station management," Castleberry agrees, "especially the news director. This is the person who sets the tone for the type of stories reporters are allowed to cover. I was able to work for several great news directors who asked me to do special reports on anything from abortion to homosexuality in the church to a series on miracles. The Lord, Himself, will open the door if we are willing to walk through it.

"Some people think that all media folks are the same, and that they are all very liberal," Castleberry explains, "but it's not true. You get people from all different backgrounds, cultures and political beliefs. But the biggest factor in deciding what goes over the air is how management wants it placed. They have the ultimate say in assignments and in how news stories are positioned. This is true for the producers, but especially for the news director.

"I was able to do some really neat series on the job. One was a feature on miracles that I didn't come up with—it was my news director. He said, 'I want a series on miracles. What can you do?' So, I called a local children's hospital, and some other folks in the medical field, and it was unbelievable the miracles that we covered.

"I did another series on homosexuality in the church. I was able to interview a guy from Exodus International, a Christian ministry to homosexuals. And I had to get the other side to be fair and balanced. But it was a conversation starter. Sometimes it's just the courage to have a conversation that can make the difference."

Humility in Interpreting the News

"I think one of the things that is important is humility in how we view how God's hand is working," Scott Baker observes. "Sometimes we look at a news story and we say, 'That's God blessing a country, or punishing a country.' I think we all need to have a great sense of humility in how we view that. How God works in many ways is truly a mystery. It is a marvelous thing to watch how it unfolds. And that is not to say that His hand is not at work and that there are not miracles in all of these things. But we need to approach that with our own sense of wonder and majesty.

"So if we see a terrible thing take place, we can pray for God's comfort and blessing and insight. But I think there needs to be a prayer asking, 'God, what are You telling us here? What is the truth? What is the meaning?'

"At a prayer breakfast in Washington, DC, Representative Gabby Giffords's husband said, 'Until recently, I had not thought very much about faith or given much attention to it.' Until tragedy strikes, many people don't. As a journalist, I've often tried to report on terrible events through how those things came into play. I was at the Murrah Building in Oklahoma City the day after it blew up. I've covered plane crashes. I've always tried to look for the story of faith and its role. I was one of the earliest to mention Todd Beamer's role on Flight 93. I looked at very specific examples of courage and faith and God's providence. I think it is a worthy thing for the news consumer to be looking for those moments of providence."

Ask, and Keep on Asking

It is also important to be persistent in our prayers for journalists. Carolyn Castleberry tells the story of a fellow journalist she prayed for and witnessed to for many years.

"A colleague of mine was a substance abuser. I co-anchored with him for 14 years, and he was an alcoholic. But he recently came to Christ. And I thought, *Wow, 14 years of prayer, where I shared with him and other believers at the station shared with him, and he thought we were idiots.* But it was Christ who delivered him. He went through lots of different programs, but at the end of the day, it was Christ that he found. So no matter how cynical and how hard people might appear on the outside, you just never know who is very close to the Kingdom."

"When you're dealing with unsaved people in the media," Jim DeSantis explains, "they cannot be moved unless they're open to be moved. A lot of times, what I pray for people who are not Christians is that someone would come across their path and bring them to the Lord. My other prayer is, 'Lord, please don't let them miss heaven.'"

"Looking at the future, it's going to be more difficult," Carolyn Castleberry believes, "especially with what's happening in the
Middle East. The financial news is only going to get more difficult. Christians are starting to ask, even on the air, is this the beginning of the end? So just pray that God's truth would come
through. And I firmly believe it does, simply because it is God's
truth. It is the word of God."

Castleberry suggests, "I would pray from the book of James.
Ask for wisdom—and don't doubt—and God will give you that
wisdom. That's a promise from Him. If you ask Him, 'How do I
present this? What should I say? Who should I interview?' God
sometimes sets up the story for you. You just ask God, 'Where do
I go? Who do I speak with? What's the best way to present this?'
Then you go out there trusting that He will show up, and He always does. It never fails. And usually, those are the best kind of
stories when you let God set it up for you.

"No matter what you do in the field of journalism, whether
you're behind the scenes, or you're a camera person or you're directing the show, if you put it before Him, saying, 'To you be the
glory, Lord,' then your level of professionalism and commitment,
and being kind to people, which is rare sometimes in that business, will shine through and cause Christ to shine in your life."

7

PRAYING THE HEADLINES

Dateline: Northern Israel, 2006 war with Hezbollah

"I want to hear the boom-boom," Dr. Pat Robertson jokingly told me (Wendy) as we rode together on a bus through northern Israel during the 2006 Israeli-Hezbollah War.

It was August 8, and the war was in its final weeks, but the Katyusha rockets being fired from southern Lebanon were still raining down on the Israelis. Many people were living in bomb shelters or had already fled south. Despite the fact that we were playing "Russian Roulette" with the Katyushas, I had a sense of excitement that only comes from being in the center of the action. Like Pat, I wanted to hear the boom-boom too—from a distance, of course.

Be careful what you wish for.

We arrived at Kiryat Shmona where Fox News had set up camp and Pat was scheduled to go "live" with *Fox and Friends*. We were on the rooftop of the building with a beautiful panoramic view of the Galilean mountains. Someone was putting on Pat's mic when suddenly and simultaneously, the bomb siren went off and I heard a loud whistle go past my head. If ever a sound was evil, it was the sound of a Katyusha whizzing past your head. Moments later, the bomb exploded in a white cloud of smoke on the hillside behind us. We rushed to the basement of the building, where we waited for the all-clear sign. We were so close to the Lebanese border that the bomb sirens were virtually useless. Normally, the siren means you have about 30 seconds to a minute to take cover. But this close to the border, the siren simply means, "Pray that you don't get hit!"

PAT ROBERTSON SPEAKING
FOR FOX & FRIENDS IN ISRAEL
(THE SMOKE FROM THE
KATYUSHA ROCKET CAN BE SEEN
ON THE MOUNTAINSIDE)

Finally, we got the all clear, and Pat did his interview with a real life understanding of the living nightmare Israelis had been going through for months.

Praying for Fox News

A few weeks before I left for Israel, in fact, even before I knew I was going, I was praying for my friend FOX News reporter Mike Tobin, who was reporting from the front lines of the war. Mike and I used to work in the Charleston, West Virginia, market at competing stations, and had become friends, but I hadn't seen or talked to him in years.

I had been glued to Fox's coverage of the war, and Mike was their main guy on the scene. Interestingly, there is a street in Virginia Beach called Tobin Street, and every time I would pass it, I would be reminded to pray for Mike and his safety and all the FOX News reporters who were on the ground. Little did I know that in just a few weeks I would be sent to Israel myself to cover the war, and come face to face with Mike.

CBN News Middle East Bureau Chief Chris Mitchell and I pulled up to an Israeli tank staging area in northern Israel, and sure enough, there was Mike. Even though I had sunglasses on, he recognized me instantly. We hugged, and I told him the story of how I'd been praying for his safety. He graciously allowed Chris and me to pray for him right there as a sea of Israeli tanks looked on.

It was a surreal moment, because one day I was praying for Mike from the safety of my home in Virginia Beach, and the next day I was with him personally in the midst of the battle. Does God care about those who are covering the news? You bet He does. And He will send you across the globe to encourage, pray and essentially be His hands and feet to those who are in the midst of battle.

Prayer from Psalm 91

Two days later, I was in the northern Israeli border town of Metula. If not for the war, it would be a perfect place to vacation or just enjoy the view of Mount Hermon and the green Galilean countryside. But there were no tourists in Metula then, only soldiers, journalists and a few innkeepers.

It was lunchtime, and my crew and I sat down next to a table of Israeli soldiers. To our surprise, most were English speaking. One was from Great Britain and another was American. They had both made Aliyah (immigration to the land of Israel) with the purpose of joining the Israeli Army and defending the Jewish nation from her vast enemies. Some of the soldiers were familiar with *The 700 Club,* which airs in the Middle East, and seemed to find comfort in the fact that a group of Christians was with them on the front lines. I opened my Bible to Psalm 91. I told one soldier, "This is what we're praying for you":

> You will not fear the terror of night, nor that arrow that flies by day. . . . For he will command his angels concerning you to guard you in all your ways; they will lift you up in their hands, so that you will not strike your foot against a stone (Ps. 91:5,11-12, *NIV*).

He thanked me and said he was familiar with the passage. As I cut my steak, I could hear the machine gun fire coming from the tanks less than a mile away. I was in the eye of the storm, surrounded by the sounds of war, yet totally at peace. Psalm 91 was coming to life for me as well:

> I will say of the LORD, "He is my refuge and my fortress, my God, in whom I trust. . . . He will cover you with his feathers, and under his wings you will find refuge. . . . A thousand may fall at your side, ten thousand at your right hand, but it will not come near you. You will only observe with your eyes and see the punishment of the wicked (Ps. 91:2,4,7-8, *NIV*).

CHRIS MITCHELL, PAT ROBERTSON AND WENDY GRIFFITH IN NORTHERN ISRAEL

As we prepared to leave, we prayed with several Israeli soldiers for God to be with them, protect them and give them victory.

I don't believe it was a coincidence that we prayed for this particular group of soldiers that was just hours away from returning to the battlefield. Only God knew what lay ahead for them. Our mission as Christians was simply to love and encourage those whom God brought across our path—and also to bless Israel. Every born-again believer has a mandate to pray for Israel and to bless the Jewish people. In the book of Genesis, God explains how we are to treat the Jewish people:

> I will bless those who bless you, and whoever curses you I will curse; and all peoples on earth will be blessed through you (Gen. 12:3, *NIV*).

> Pray for the peace of Jerusalem: "May they prosper who love you" (Ps. 122:6, *NKJV*).

Praying the Headlines

Whether you're literally on the front lines of war or in the comfort of your own home, when you pray the news, you work with the Lord to see captives set free. Our cooperation with God in the establishment of His kingdom on earth is an amazing mystery. Sometimes we may wonder why God chooses to use us to help carry out His will on the earth. We may wonder, *God, why don't You use the angels? You still have two-thirds of them, and they are much more obedient than we are.* Yet, as we grow in our walk with the Lord, we realize that in His sovereign wisdom, He has chosen to use frail human beings to carry out His will on the earth.

Intercession is a dynamic spiritual partnership where the Holy Spirit places a burden on our hearts and then empowers us to pray—even giving us the proper words to utter in every situation, as He did with Wendy in Israel. If we are to co-labor with the Lord in prayer, it is vital that we remain sensitive to the leading of His Spirit. Sometimes that can be a moment-by-moment leading. We must remain humble so that we can willingly move into intercession at a moment's notice, and then pray the will of the Father as the Spirit leads us.

Author and journalist Marcia Moston tells the story of praying that the Lord would intervene in a crisis. During a major house renovation, without a job and far from friends, Marcia was at a low point. Sections of the Sunday newspaper lay scattered among the tools and stacks of sheetrock in her home. As she scanned the articles, one headline caught her attention: "Hostage: Here We Are Living Like the Living Dead."[1]

The article described a letter and video of an American missionary, Ingrid Betancourt, held hostage for six years in the Columbian jungle. "I thought about her physical discomfort," Marcia explains, "and I thought about her despair. I ripped the article out and stuffed it in my Bible."

Every night, when the stress of her own life kept her from sleep at 3:00 A.M., she remembered Ingrid Betancourt and the American hostages. "From between my soft sheets, I lifted prayers for those sleeping in hammocks strung between trees. On December 6, my journal entry read: 'For those captives losing heart—to Him who is able to do exceedingly more—please give them hope, Lord. This day, break the power of the captors and set the captives free.'"

For months, whenever Marcia's despair clamored for attention, she prayed for the band of captives in a Columbian jungle. "I wondered how I would ever know what happened to them and when I should stop praying for them."

A few weeks before Christmas, after six years of captivity in that jungle thousands of miles away, Ingrid Betancourt gave up hope of ever being set free. Her unanswered prayers settled back on her as she folded herself in her hammock cocoon and let go of the will to live. The proof-of-life letter she had written to her family never reached its destination—or so she thought.

She was unaware that some militia had been captured and the letter was released to the press. She was unaware of an army deep in the jungle, rehearsing a rescue. And she was unaware that God had roused intercessors around the world, including Marcia Moston.

On December 7, 2007, a world away, a news article about Ingrid Betancourt once again caught Marcia's attention. She clipped it and stuck it in her Bible. Marcia says, "Night after restless night, from between my sheets, I prayed for a woman who had lost hope."

The next day, December 8, 2007, in the depths of a Colombian jungle, Ingrid heard about the rescued letters. She wrote, "For the first time in six months, I wanted to eat. . . . I had a thirst for life again."

Six months later, on a warm July morning, coffee cup in hand, Marcia turned on her computer. "The Windows screen cleared," she remembers, "and the local news page opened. There in bold letters across my screen was the headline: 'Betancourt Freed.'" God had heard Marcia crying out from the midst of her own emotional pain and had brought freedom to a captive thousands of miles away in answer to her prayers.[2]

Just as God used Marcia to pray from the headlines, so too He will use you as you follow the leading of the Spirit. The rest of this chapter is about areas of influence that the Lord has used others to pray for—and that He may place on your heart as you pray the news.

Praying for Those in Authority

In order to live in a civilized world, we must have authority structures and government. The apostle Paul urged the church to pray for civil authorities so that the Gospel could be carried forward in peace: "First of all, then, I urge that entreaties and prayers, petitions and thanksgivings, be made on behalf of all men, for kings and all who are in authority, so that we may lead a tranquil and quiet life in all godliness and dignity" (1 Tim. 2:1-2).

More than ever, it is vital that we pray for people in all levels of government—including our president or prime minister; the congress or parliament; the courts system; our governors; and our state and local governments. We can also pray for local officials like our school board members or other civic bodies.

How can we effectively pray for the nation? Dutch Sheets, internationally known speaker and author of *Intercessory Prayer*, says that we should pray in this way:

1. Pray that many in the church sense the need for humility and repentance.
2. Pray that the church is able to respond to a national crisis with great wisdom.
3. Ask for a turning of our nation back to God.
4. Ask for God's mercy to triumph over judgment.
5. Pray that our president and other government leaders move with great wisdom.
6. Pray for comfort in our nation and that each person recognizes his or her great spiritual need.
7. Forgive those who have wronged us and pray for justice to evildoers.
8. Continue to pray for the salvation of the Muslim world.

Dutch reminds us that God wants to give witness to the world that Jesus is still alive today. "If we make the right decisions in this nation," says Dutch, "we will see a great return of the miraculous." God will work miracles in our homes, schools, offices and in the streets. He will set people free and deliver them. God has strategies for us to implement to turn this nation around. Anyone who is listening to hear a word from the Lord is in a position to reveal to us these strategies. When these plans are followed, they release an authority from the Lord that opens doors of breakthrough, revival and healing.[3]

Praying for the Military

Author and intercessor Janet Teitsort has written much on prayer for our military since her grandson entered the service. She has turned her concern for this grandchild into prayers that she shares in various media outlets. As you pray the news for our military, you may want to use her "Prayer for a Soldier":

Lord, today I lift up the soldier who is continents away fighting in a war that seems to have no end. Lord, he's only twenty-one, and already he has seen more horror than I can even imagine. Life picked him up right out of high school with only a taste of college, and hurled him into the reality of war in the new millennium. Dreams to be fulfilled, serving his country, and righting things in a "world gone wrong" were utmost in his thoughts. But what a transition, Lord!

Sounds of mortar pepper his nights and days, causing loss of hearing. The harsher reality is that sometimes he and his buddies are showered with the shrapnel, taking a hit. God, hold him when he loses a buddy. Hold him when he's so scared that life moves in slow motion. Hear his silent prayers, his plea for Your help. Give him strength to lift that buddy and carry him out of harm's way. Give him courage to wipe his tears, unashamed, and keep moving.

Lord, he's in hostile territory every moment. Protect him and his company from hidden enemies. Guide their decisions—cause them to make the right decision every moment—to turn in the right direction. Give them discernment from lying enemies, from those who would do them harm. Help them to work as a team, dear Jesus. Surround them with Your angels of protection. May their commanders look to You for guidance.

Grant him sleep in the moments he has to rest. Protect him from sickness. Help him not to be homesick to the point that it makes him unable to focus. Guard his mind in Christ Jesus—he who has seen evil in its cruelest forms. Protect his mind, his sanity, Lord. Help him to hold it all together. Help him not to lose sight of the big picture— the holding back of evil so mankind can live in peace.

And Jesus, fill him with the assurance that You are with him every moment. Encourage him with thoughts of us who are at home. Help him to picture us praying for him, remembering what he is about, and that always, we are proud of him and thank him for his gallant fight for peace.

Now, Lord, You who trained King David's hand for battle, equip this young soldier. Be his fortress, his hiding place. Deliver him from seen and unseen enemies. Surround him with ministering angels and those who will do battle on his behalf. Protect him from every possible harm in this foreign land.

I praise You, Lord. I praise You who are able to do all of this and more. I entrust this soldier, this boy who is now a man, to Your watch care. Thy will be done. In Jesus' Name, amen.[4]

Praying for the Weather

Jesus demonstrated His power over the wind and the waves. If we have His authority to do the same things He did, and even greater things (see John 14:12), then we can pray for the weather as well.

It was August 29, 2005, and New Orleans was bracing itself for a Category 5 monster storm named Katrina. My crew and I (Wendy) were on one of the last flights allowed to land in New Orleans that day. Even the airport attendants looked at us like we were crazy. But, for me, going in to a place when everyone else is going out is part of the job, and I like being where the action is.

In a series of miraculous events, we were able to rent a four-wheel drive vehicle and get one of the few remaining hotel rooms left in the city, a corner room on the seventh floor of the Hilton Hotel, just a few feet from the Mississippi River and not far from Lake Pontchartrain. In other words, we were surrounded by water in a city that already sits below sea level. While many people were frantically trying to leave New Orleans by any means possible, my colleagues, CBN News reporter Charlene Israel, and cameraman Jim Lea, and I felt remarkably peaceful. Perhaps it was just the calm before the storm, but we had a sense that we were exactly where we were supposed to be and that this would be no ordinary assignment.

We were right.

After we shot our quintessential "blowing in the wind, rain pelting your face" hurricane stand-up, we hunkered down for the night. Fortunately, our room faced inside, toward the atrium of the hotel. Another major blessing was that despite the storm pressing down on us, we had electricity all night long. This meant we were glued to the weather channel as we watched this incredibly large blob on the radar move ever closer to The Crescent City.

As we watched, a jolt of fear went through me. *What if Katrina makes a direct hit on the city? What if this hotel isn't strong enough to withstand her winds? What if I have put myself and my crew in serious danger?* One thing was certain: It was too late to change plans. We were in New Orleans for what appeared to be the storm of the century. Jim, who had weathered many previous hurricanes, fell asleep on a cot and was even snoring. Charlene and I were in separate beds. But around 3:00 A.M., the hotel started creaking violently and the water in the bathtub (we filled up the tub so we would have water to flush the toilets after the storm hit) was sloshing up and down the sides of the tub.

Curled up in the covers, I prayed, "Lord, please don't let this be a direct hit." I heard in my spirit, "It's done." In other words, I felt the Lord was reassuring me that it would not be a direct hit, which could literally mean the difference between life and death for many, including us! Around that time, Charlene jumped into bed with me, and we sang praise songs and thanked God for His mighty hand of protection upon us and the people of New Orleans. I don't remember falling asleep that night, but I do remember we both felt that we were supposed to be there.

The next morning we discovered why.

The Morning After

Around 11:00 A.M., although it was still raining and windy, the storm had passed enough for us to leave the hotel and assess the damage. But the walk through the hotel's parking garage remains one of my scariest Katrina moments. The storm had knocked loose the garage ceiling. What looked like gigantic, jagged, metal razors swung precariously from the ceiling and were still being blown around by the wind. Praying not to be sliced in half, I ran to our vehicle as fast as I could. After making it out of the parking garage alive, I was ready for anything.

The French Quarter had a lot of downed trees and power lines but didn't look that bad. The radio was reporting major flooding. We drove up the I-10 ramp and that's when we saw it. There was water up to the housetops, with people on their roofs frantically waving their hands in hopes of being rescued. The only people out at this point were rescue workers and a few media.

One of the first people we met was the assistant police chief. After he gave us an interview, we asked him if we could pray for him. He bowed his head and a tear washed over his cheek. No one—not the victims, and not even the rescue workers—was prepared to handle this catastrophe. People needed prayer. Suddenly, our mission became clear. God had given us access because we were media; but our real mission was to pray and bring the light and hope of Jesus Christ into the midst of their suffering.

Rescued

The next day, things took a turn for the worse when the canal walls burst and water started spilling over the levees and into the streets of New Orleans. As the water inched its way up Canal Street toward our hotel, the looting began, and my cameraman even had a knife pulled on him as he tried to capture the action. When we got back to the hotel and were in our room, someone was banging on the doors, saying, "If you can leave the city, leave now. Don't wait!" The water was closing in on the hotel, and a spirit of lawlessness had taken over the city. The looters outnumbered the police, and it no longer felt safe or wise to stay.

Later, when we reflected on those events, we all felt the person who knocked on the hotel door might have been an angel, because we never saw him.

As we prepared to make our escape, four people from New York who had been in New Orleans for a convention but were now stranded, asked if we could give them a ride. My first thought was no way can we fit four extra people, including two pretty large men, and all of our camera gear and luggage into one vehicle. But lives were more important than luggage. So we dumped our suitcases and put our clothes in plastic bags that we could sit on or hold on our laps, and took off.

As we drove out of town, we saw people wading through waist-high water carrying a few belongings on their shoulders. Some of them looked strangely calm but were probably still in shock. We drove our new friends to the nearest airport a couple hours away and said goodbye. One of the ladies was named Wendy, like me. When I got back to CBN, she sent me a beautiful silver necklace with a little angel on it. She said we were her angels that day and that we had rescued them.

Truly, it was God who rescued them. We were just along for the ride.

Hurricane Isabel

Author Lynetta Jordan tells how the local news was forecasting that her hometown of Edenton, North Carolina, was in the direct path of Hurricane Isabel. It was a fierce category 3 storm, threatening destructive winds and catastrophic flooding. People filled the grocery and department stores, buying the necessary nonperishable food, water, ice, flashlights and batteries. Lynetta says, "My family, with rich Christian heritage, also prepared spiritually with fervent prayer."

Stubborn Hurricane Isabel stayed steady on her course and refused to change. "News reports continued to announce that she was moving directly toward us," Lynetta says. "I thought it would be wise to make natural preparation in case the storm hit us, but I still chose to believe the report of the Lord. I was confident that God heard me and would answer on time.

"The Goliath of a storm marched into northeastern North Carolina with fury. Torrential rains and whipping winds crashed against my parents' two-story home. I was safe with my sister and her family there, while Mom and Dad had journeyed less than a mile to stay with my grandparents to ensure their safety.

"While we still had phone service, we called and checked on each other periodically. But one call from my mother was different. Her voice was no longer light. Mom had been shaken. She told me that two towering pine trees had fallen down onto the roof. Thank God, Mom and Dad were not hurt. But where were my grandparents?

"Mom said that she had called the ambulance, but they were unable to venture out in this, the fiercest part of the storm. Seconds felt like hours as I waited to hear. Then Mom told me that she had moved Grandma and Granddaddy from their bedroom to the den only minutes before the trees fell. My grandparents, a retired pastor and first lady, were fine.

"I was so very grateful for God's marvelous hand of protection, showing Himself mighty for us once again. I started crying, rejoicing and thanking God with the phone still in my hand. He kept all of us safe and spared my parents' and grandparents' lives in the midst of the storm."

When the storm was over, Lynetta and her sister drove to her grandparents' home. "I smelled wet pine as I approached their bedroom door. When I saw the trees and looked up and saw the now blue and clearing sky through the hole in the ceiling, I was in absolute awe of God. One tree had fallen on Granddaddy's desk, and the other had fallen at the foot of their bed—exactly where they would have been sitting and resting.

"El Shaddai saved all of their lives! Though it was two weeks before all power was restored, there was still light shining bright in the hearts of God's people in Edenton, North Carolina. Not one life was lost, including the lives of my dear grandparents. I was so grateful that the effectual, fervent prayers of the righteous had availed much."[5]

Praying for Our Cities

Donna Collins Tinsley had to overcome tremendous challenges in life through the power of the cross. As a survivor of childhood sexual abuse, and whose first husband was a pedophile, Donna had great compassion for those trapped in sexual sin. "I pray the news and sometimes get involved with people I read about in the newspaper," she says. One local news story that grabbed her attention was about a woman serial killer.

"I found myself drawn to the series written in our local newspaper about Aileen Wuornos, and had compassion on her. I hated the crimes she had committed, and I felt a lot of pain for her victims; but I always wondered what she had endured as a child to lead her to this point." Donna explains that studies have shown again and again that most women who work as prostitutes have been physically or sexually abused as children. Fifty-seven percent reported a history of childhood sexual abuse by an average of three perpetrators.[6]

"I always wondered if the right person had shined the light of Jesus on Aileen Wuornos, would she have gone a different route? When I see a woman working the streets, I always think, *That is somebody's daughter. What if she were yours? Wouldn't you still love her and pray for her? Wouldn't you hope for the best and pray that she will come to her senses?*"

A few years after the *Daytona Beach News Journal* did a series of special reports on Aileen, Donna saw an ad in a smaller newspaper from a woman named Aida who wanted to open a home for ministry to prostitutes. "It led me to go meet her," Donna says. "When I saw the beauty in her face as she described what she wanted to do with an older home she had found in the middle of the red light district, I was captivated with the dream. 'Heaven's Garden' was born in her heart, and I felt a kindred spirit to Aida. I knew that if Aileen Wuornos had been alive at that time, she would have had a chance at recovery through a ministry such as this one."

Through this recovery ministry to prostitutes in the heart of Daytona, the dream lives on. The home has been restored to help women from any background, not just prostitution. It is labeled as a "Sober House." As one of the few recovery houses in Florida for women, it provides a structured and stable living environment to aid women in achieving their recovery goals.

Praying Against Crime

Michael Roberts was 53 and homeless when he was brutally murdered by a group of teens who found him in his outdoor camp and beat him repeatedly with logs and their fists. "Although I didn't know him," Donna remembers, "I attended his memorial service at a local homeless shelter. So many people were moved by the violence of his death. He was just a man who lived in the woods rather than be a burden on his family. One woman shared at the service how for years she was afraid of the homeless on the streets of Daytona. But now she looks into their eyes with compassion because of his death."

This crime prompted the people of eastern Florida to create The STAR Family Shelter. According to executive director Lisa Hamilton, at last count, the homeless coalition listed 2,155 homeless people, both sheltered and unsheltered.

"Praying the news has also prompted me to write to the mother of a daughter who is awaiting trial for the murder of her little girl," Donna explains. "It led me to pray for the grandmother of the little girl who has not been found. I have a special place in my heart for hurting mothers and grandmothers—maybe because for years, I had a daughter who was leading a street life, and I know how it feels. By the grace of God, she is clean and sober now; but I believe that we need to remember our experiences of pain and reach out to others in prayer."

Donna says that she finds herself praying the news often. "Sometimes it stirs me to write. Sometimes it stirs me to go. Sometimes it stirs me to serve. But the news I hear always stirs me to pray. I believe one person praying can make a difference in our world."[7]

Author Jeanne Gowen Dennis tells how one quiet afternoon, her almost five-year-old daughter was watching television with her when a news flash interrupted the program. The nightmare all parents dread and pray they never experience had just occurred only 10 miles from their home. A man had brazenly abducted a three-year-old girl from her front yard, right in front of other playing children.

"No, Lord," Jeanne prayed silently. "Not that. Not here." Then she started praying for the little girl's parents—her mother who found out the horrifying news at work, and her father who had been just feet away inside the house. *How helpless he must have felt,* Jeanne thought. *How riddled with guilt that he hadn't been able to protect her, to stop the monster who now might be harming his baby.*

Her prayer continued. "Jesus, please don't let that little girl die." It seemed like most kidnapping cases with strangers as abductors ended with tiny, mutilated bodies and heartbroken parents. "Not this time, Lord," she cried. "Please!"

"It concerned me that my daughter, Christine, had heard about the kidnapping. I wondered if it would frighten her, and I knew she would ask me every day if the little girl had been rescued. If the child were later found dead, how could I tell her? What would it do to her tender faith that had just begun to grow?"

But little Christine said, "I want to pray for the little girl. I know God can find her so her mommy won't be sad anymore."

Jeanne recalls, "Christine's faith, stronger and purer than mine, had not become tainted by unanswered prayers or disappointing outcomes. Whereas I, like most other adults, wondered at the sovereign will of God—why He sometimes protected, saved or healed people and other times didn't. My little daughter and I prayed together. Then I warned her about trusting strangers.

"Christine and I prayed several times in the next couple of days," Jeanne says. "But by Wednesday evening, authorities' concerns grew. The little girl had not been wearing much clothing, and nighttime temperatures in the late summer could be dangerously cool, especially in the nearby foothills and mountains. I prayed more earnestly. 'Lord, my daughter believes You are going to help the police find that little girl alive. Please reward her childlike trust in You—and help me to have faith as strong as hers.'"

Thursday morning, Jeanne was upstairs when she heard her daughter yelling, "They found the little girl!"

"What? Is she all right?" Jeanne stumbled downstairs two steps at a time, her heart full of hope but still tinged with doubt that the child had been found alive and unharmed. "We watched footage of the mother screaming as she was told the child had been found alive. She frantically climbed into a car so she could be rushed to the hospital to see her daughter."

WENDY GRIFFITH AND MIKE TOBIN

The story that unfolded throughout the day showed the miraculous hand of God so clearly that Jeanne knew He had responded not only to her and her daughter's prayers, but also to those of the hundreds of people across the country who had prayed the news for the abducted child and her family. That morning, a woman who had been hiking and bird watching in the mountains with her husband had to use the bathroom. They made a wrong turn and ended up in a park that had closed for the season. She used an outhouse and then heard a child calling for her mommy. After searching and calling to the child, they found a little blonde girl standing in sewage in the pit below the outhouse. She wanted a drink and told them she lived there.

Apparently, the abductor knew the park would be empty at that time of year. He figured the elements and sewage would do his dirty work for him, and the child's body most likely would never be found. But this evil man hadn't reckoned on the power of God, the gracious God who answers prayers. Lori Poland, the little girl the man had left for dead, had to be treated for exposure and dehydration as well as for infections in her feet from the sewage. She had to heal from the abuse she had suffered at the man's hand, but she survived. Even at the tender age of three, she identified her kidnapper, Robert Thiret, from a photograph. He later confessed. Lori grew up to be the first in her family to graduate from college—an optimistic, accomplished young woman with a heart for sexually abused children.

"My daughter's faith never wavered during the three days we prayed," Jeanne proclaims, "and the loving heavenly Father extended His grace to her, even as He sent help to little Lori. Christine has grown into a woman of strong faith. Now she is passing on that heritage to her own children—childlike trust in the One to whom all glory is due, the God who answers prayers even when we pray for people we've never met . . . except through the news."[8]

Praying for the Economy

Here is another prayer from Janet Teitsort, for our national economy. It can also be prayed for your regional or local economy as you intercede for God's financial blessing on your community.

> Almighty God, we pray for the economy of this nation, for it seems that we, the people, in our humanness, are helpless to fix it. Many are unemployed, devastated by cutbacks in businesses and schools. Long lines of unemployment are formed, jobs are sought, but to no avail.
>
> Gambling is on the rise, as people seek a quick fix. Some are stressed beyond their limits and resort to embezzlement or some illegal means to provide an income.
>
> Father, give us strength of character to save, to learn to do without in order to pay as we go. Teach us that we don't have to have instant gratification. Help us once again to enjoy a simple picnic instead of having to have a vacation that costs thousands [of dollars]. Move in the hearts of the people to seek their riches in You.
>
> Teach us the guidelines from Your Word on money management and give us the desire and ability to follow them. Help us, Father, to handle our money in ways that please You.[9]

Taking the Territory

One of the things the Bible makes clear about God is that He is into geography. When God brought the Children of Israel to the Promised Land, He first gave them the condition that they were to obey the Law He had given them through Moses. He gave them the promise that He would drive out all the nations from before them. And then God made an amazing declaration that harkens back to the dominion He gave to man in the Garden. He extended that dominion to the Children of Israel in the Promised Land, under this Sinaitic Covenant:

Every place on which the sole of your foot treads shall be yours (Deut. 11:24).

God repeated this promise after Moses died and Joshua became the leader. Even though this promise was made to natural Israel, it is a type and a shadow of what God has promised for spiritual Israel—you and me—under the New Covenant. God's ultimate purpose is to restore the world to the same order that was in the Garden of Eden. He desires for us to co-labor with Him in prayer and Kingdom ministry until . . .

The earth will be filled with the knowledge of the glory of the LORD, as the waters cover the sea (Hab. 2:14).

So God wants to use us to claim the territory He directs us to take in Jesus' name. If the Spirit of God directs us to pray a certain way, or to lay claim to a certain place or thing in the spirit realm, we need to move forward in faith—even if we may appear foolish in the eyes of the world.

Years ago, I (Craig) learned this concept from my pastor, who led us in various prayer walks to "take the city" for God. The local news was filled with stories about the sagging economy and the resulting poverty, crime and other social ills. In those years, our church prayed the news for new life and new businesses to flood into the downtown area. We also prayed against crime, poverty and corruption in government. We rejoiced as businesses expanded and new companies were started, breathing life into this industrial city. We were amazed when corrupt government officials were driven from office. In one poignant example, we saw a seedy nightclub that had been notorious for crime, drugs and prostitution burn to the ground, never to be rebuilt (thankfully, no one was hurt).

During those years, the news was filled with stories of factories closing and companies moving operations overseas. The Lord began to speak to me during my daily prayer time about specific places in the city that He wanted me to pray for. In one instance, He gave me the assignment to walk around a large industrial complex that once had been a thriving earth-moving machine manufacturer. This factory covered two city blocks and had sat empty and deteriorating for nearly a decade. God told me to walk around the entire complex, placing my hands on the four corners of the factory and praying for it to come back to life. He instructed me to take authority over a spirit of poverty and a spirit of blight. He had me do this several times in the course of one year, each time placing my hands on the four corners of the building and declaring that new life and new business would spring forth from this place. Every time I drove past this factory, I would repeat this declaration of new life and I would bind the spirit of blight.

After a year of praying in this manner, I noticed that one small business had moved into one tiny part of the factory. The rest of the complex remained shuttered. But like a tiny green shoot sprouting from the ground, the new life that I had prayed for had suddenly emerged. Within a few months, another new business leased a different part of the factory. Then another section opened up, then another. And then yet another, until the entire complex was filled, not with one company, but with several different companies that occupied various parts of the once vacant complex. Suddenly the entire factory was alive again and bursting with activity as trucks and cars buzzed in and out carrying people, materials and finished products ready for shipment to the world.

New Life in "Dry Bones"

There were not that many multi-story buildings in our downtown, so it was always a thrill when a new one was built, and a tragedy when an old, beautiful building was torn down. For decades, one of the crown jewels of downtown was a several stories building called the Boston Store, which was like a small town version of

Macy's department store in New York. As a teenager, the "in" thing to do was to go downtown and meet your friends under the large clock in the center of the Boston Store. This became such a part of Erie's culture that the management ran ads declaring, "Meet under the clock at the Boston Store."

When I was a small child, the Boston Store was always decorated to the hilt for Christmas and buzzing with activity and excitement. My earliest memory of sitting on Santa's lap at Christmas time was at the Boston Store in downtown Erie, Pennsylvania.

But like so many cities across America, Erie's downtown took a tremendous economic hit when the modern mall was built out in the suburbs. The news media related stories of retailers who moved in droves from the inner city, with expensive and inadequate parking, to the new mega-mall with acres of free parking. Within a very short time, the once bustling downtown became a virtual ghost town. It wasn't long before the Boston Store closed its doors forever.

For more than a decade this once luxurious landmark stood empty and boarded up. Pigeons flew in and out of windows broken by vandals.

During my prayer time, I once again sensed the leading of the Holy Spirit to pray that new life would come to the Boston Store. I drove downtown, parked my car on the now quiet street, walked over to the empty high rise and laid my hands on the brick exterior. "Heavenly Father," I prayed out loud, "You have called me to speak life to this building. So in obedience to Your leading, I declare life to the Boston Store, in Jesus' name. I curse and bind the spirit of blight and poverty and release Your blessing on this property. God, nothing is impossible to You, so I pray that You would resurrect this building and breathe Your life into it, in Jesus' name."

When I was finished, I got back into my car and looked up to the top of the building. "Lord," I prayed, "You can make these dry bones live." As I did with the factory, every time I drove past the Boston Store, I would speak life into it and curse a spirit of poverty and blight. Sometimes the Lord would bring the building to mind and I would pray right there on the spot that God would bring restoration to that beautiful landmark.

Then, one day, after several years of prayer, I was driving past the Boston Store and saw a sign in the window for new shops and apartments to be opened in the coming months. My heart rejoiced at this sign of new birth. Then I received word that my brother and sister were invited to do a Christian concert on stage for a New Year's Eve celebration at the Boston Store. Our family and friends joyfully agreed that we would "meet under the clock!"

I spoke to my mother on the phone recently, and she told me that she was on her way that night to a Bible study in downtown Erie. I was filled with joy when she told me that the Bible study was being held in the apartment of a friend . . . in the Boston Store!

8

PRAYING THE
NEWS TO REVIVAL

"These gates lead to the presence of the LORD, and the godly enter there. I thank you for answering my prayer and giving me victory!" (Ps. 118:20-21, *NLT*).

Former First Lady Barbara Bush had a friend who told her that she prayed for her son George every day. The mother to a president replied, "Well, please continue, because he feels your prayers. He tells me he feels your prayers."

Her friend responded, "I know that's true. I had a mastectomy operation, and all my friends got a prayer group going. They prayed for me. When it was over and I was well, when they stopped praying . . . I felt that they had stopped praying."

"I believe that," Mrs. Bush answered. "The power of those prayers was so strong that she felt it, and when the cancer left, she felt them stop praying. I believe you can feel it when people are praying for you."[1]

The Lord had people praying for George W. Bush even before he was president. In 1997, three years before the election, God prompted Julie Arduini to read the book of Esther in the Old Testament. When she prayed, the phrase from Esther's story "for such a time as this" stood out to her for the 2000 election. "My journal contained notes from Esther," she remembers, "as well as a directive from the Lord to 'pray against wolves in sheep's clothing.'"

The margin in the 2000 presidential election was razor-thin. Many people were praying the news during that tense season. As people across America watched their television sets, the pivotal state of Florida was awarded to Al Gore. Then only a short time later, the network suddenly reversed itself and put Florida into the Bush column, giving him enough votes to become president of the United States. For several tense days, votes were being counted and "hanging chads" were being examined across Florida as God's people prayed for His will to be done.

Julie recalls, "Those divisive weeks between election night and the day George Bush was declared the presidential winner were deep prayer times for me. Looking back, I wonder if then Florida Secretary of State Katherine Harris was a contemporary Esther, thrust into the spotlight for 'such a time as this.' Only God knows what He meant by the wolves, but just from reading news updates there was certainly a plethora of lawyers and political heavyweights trying to jockey for position."[2]

When the Supreme Court ruled in favor of George W. Bush, making him the forty-third President of the United States, many people believed it was an answer to the prayers of hundreds of thousands who were praying the news in that tumultuous time.

Prayer Brings Revival and Affects the Outcome of Our Times

Writing on the subject of prayer, Martin Luther declared, "No one can believe how powerful prayer is and what it can effect, except those who have learned it by experience. . . . I know, whenever I have prayed earnestly, that I have been heard and have obtained more than I prayed for. God sometimes delays, but He always comes."[3]

The faith-filled intercession of God's people praying the news can change the course of history for good. Many times history records great changes in the course of what is happening in any given time as a result of an outpouring of the Holy Spirit in revival. And in almost every case, that revival was a result of concerted and ongoing prayer on the part of God's people. Learning how God released revival as a result of dedicated prayer in the past can give us faith to believe that He can and will do it in our day as we pray the news.

The news ultimately will change for the good when revival comes.

The Haystack Revival

On a Saturday afternoon in August 1806, five students from Williams College in Williamstown, Massachusetts, gathered in what was then known as Sloan's Meadow. They met to pray and discuss theology, and soon the conversation turned to the spiritual needs of those living in foreign countries. Suddenly a violent thunderstorm arose and they ran to take shelter in the lee of a haystack where they continued to pray. This gathering came to be called "The Haystack Prayer Meeting."

A first-year student, Samuel Mills, was the son of a Congregational minister who had a passion for the lost in the nations of the world. In the shelter of the haystack, he spoke to his classmates of Asia, a subject he was studying in geography class. He then revealed what was for some Protestants of that time and place a radical idea—sending missionaries to take the gospel to far-off lands.

Filled with the zeal of the Holy Spirit, Mills proposed to the five at the haystack that they be the ones to go. The Haystack Missionary Movement was born as the rain poured down from heaven, both literally and spiritually.

Mills continued as the driving force behind the movement during its early years. Still at Williams in 1808, he and other students formalized their plan to become missionaries after they completed their studies. They named themselves "The Society of the Brethren," a group chartered "to effect, in the person of its members, a mission to the heathen." Mills and two other members of the Brethren continued their studies at Andover Seminary outside Boston, where they found great excitement among Andover students for the idea of mission. In 1810, Mills and three Andover students persuaded some of New England's leading Congregational clergy to organize a foreign missionary society, which soon became The American Board of Commissioners for Foreign Missions.

The first five missionaries were ordained in 1812. Over the next seven years, the board sent the first American Christian missionaries to India, Ceylon, the Cherokee and Choctaw nations, the Sandwich Islands and even to the Holy Land.[4]

In its first fifty years, the ABCFM sent out more than 1,250 missionaries around the world. When they reached the mission field, they immediately set out to translate the Bible and make it available in written form. They often found tribes without a written language. In addition, they built educational systems, and were sometimes called upon to advise foreign governments. After 150 years, the American Board had sent out nearly 5,000 missionaries to 34 different fields.[5]

"There are tens of thousands of Christians all over the world who understand themselves to have become Christians as a result of the Haystack Prayer Meeting," said Williams College Chaplain, Richard Spalding. A 12-foot granite monument erected in 1867 marks the spot of the prayer meeting. Capped by a globe, it stands on what is known as Mission Park on the Williams College campus. The monument announces the location as the birthplace of American foreign missions and declares that "The Field is the World."[6]

It all began with the prayer of five young people committed to taking the gospel to the people of the nations—just as Jesus commanded.

Layman's Prayer Revival

There was a time in America when the streets of New York City, Washington, DC, and other major cities across the nation were nearly deserted every day at noon as people joined together to pray. It happened in 1857, when the leadership at Fulton Street Church in New York City saw a sharp decline in attendance. They called on Jeremiah Lanphier, a former merchant with no formal theological training, to lead the effort to reach the unchurched of the city. Lanphier wasn't sure how to proceed, so he organized a noonday prayer meeting. He printed up notices and handed them out on the streets of New York. Lanphier announced that he was a city missionary and there was going to be an open prayer meeting.

On the day of the meeting, Lanphier waited at the Fulton Street Church.

No one showed up, so he began to pray on his own. Twenty minutes later, he heard someone coming up the stairs to join him.

In this first meeting, only a handful of people came for intercession, but Lanphier refused to be discouraged.

At the next meeting, a few more people joined him. Soon the room was filled with people praying for the city. The prayer meeting grew from one room to two rooms, then to three rooms filled with intercessors. Eventually, the church sanctuary was bursting with people praying for revival.

In the following months, noonday prayer meetings sprang up all across the city. Soon factories were blowing the lunch whistle at 11:55 A.M. to give workers the chance to rush to the nearest church to pray for an hour. Churches of all denominations were filled with people praying on their lunch break.

This caught the attention of the media. The editor of the *New York Herald Tribune* was looking out of his window at a few minutes before noon and was shocked to see men running from their places of business, bumping into one another and then disappearing into churches. He sent a reporter to investigate. The journalist returned later that day and announced, "They are all praying."

The next day the editor sent out a team of reporters to cover the whole city. They came back and reported that up to 15,000 people were praying across the city. The *Herald Tribune* began publishing stories of the prayer meetings, and within a short time more than 25,000 people were interceding for the city. The more stories the paper published, the bigger the meetings became.

Soon more than 40,000 people were praying through the lunch hour across New York City. Prayer meetings organized by lay leadership spread like wildfire throughout the United States. Noontime prayer meetings were being reported in Pittsburgh, Cleveland, Chicago, Denver and Los Angeles. Across the country, people would read the New York papers and then revival would break out in their cities.

By 1859, more than one million unchurched Americans were won to Christ as a result of the Layman's Prayer Revival. God poured out His Spirit, preparing America for one of its darkest chapters in history. Only two years later, the Civil War erupted in the United States, and tens of thousands of men were slain. Many of these men were prepared to meet their Savior during this out-pouring of revival before they went into the battle.[7]

In the dreary first year of the American Civil War, when it seemed the nation would be permanently divided over the issue of slavery, the abolitionist and poet Julia Ward Howe paid a visit to Abraham Lincoln in Washington, DC. As she walked through the city, she heard a regiment of soldiers singing the popular tune "John Brown's Body" as they marched.

That night, Howe awoke with the tune playing in her mind. Sitting in near darkness, she scribbled out the verses. The song quickly became the anthem of the Union during the Civil War— "The Battle Hymn of the Republic":

> Mine eyes have seen the glory of the coming of the Lord
> He is trampling out the vintage where the grapes of
>   wrath are stored
> He hath loosed the fateful lightning of His terrible swift sword
> His truth is marching on.

Whose truth is the song referring to? God's truth. What is that truth? That God desires all those in slavery to go free! Scripture tells us that Christ came to loose the chains of those enslaved— both physically and spiritually. Jesus made this declaration in the Gospels as He began His earthly ministry:

> The Spirit of the LORD is upon me, for he has anointed me
> to bring Good News to the poor. He has sent me to pro-claim that captives will be released, that the blind will see,
> that the oppressed will be set free (Luke 4:18, NLT).

And this truth is also the mandate of those called to pray the news—to loose those trapped in bondage to sin. Intercessors prayed fervently in the Layman's Prayer Revival to prepare the nation for the coming tragedy of the Civil War. So, in our generation, we must pick up this banner of prayer and contend for those caught in the spiritual slavery of our times.

Praying John Hyde

Another man of God who later caught the vision to take the gospel to the nations was John Nelson Hyde of Carthage, Illinois. His father, Rev. Smith Harris Hyde, was a Presbyterian minister who had prayed fervently that God would raise up missionaries from America. God answered that prayer through his own son.

John's elder brother, Edmund, attended seminary with him. Edmund dreamt of being a preacher, and traveled to minister in Montana, where he unexpectedly died. John had always admired his brother, and Edmund's death brought John to a place of deep soul-searching regarding his own calling to be a missionary. He came to believe that God was calling him to India.[8]

John made the decision from that moment to give himself to prayer and study. The more he gave himself to time alone with God, the clearer and greater his vision became. He also spent countless hours learning the language. It was to the Punjab that Hyde felt led to begin his lifetime of missionary endeavor. At the time of his posting, in 1892, he was one of only five missionaries in a territory of nearly one million non-Christians.[9]

Progress was slow but measured. In a letter to his seminary after his first year in India, Hyde wrote: "Yesterday eight low-caste persons were baptized at one of the villages. It seems a work of God in which man, even as an instrument, was used in a very small degree. Pray for us. I learn to speak the language very, very slowly: can only talk a little in public or in conversation."

Hyde's inability to master the complex native languages was a result of his partial deafness. But to the dismay of mission authorities, rather than focus on language study, he devoted most of his time to Bible study and prayer. In time, however, Hyde gained fluency in the language, though he continued in his zeal for Scripture and prayer.

In 1895, Hyde worked with another missionary, and a small revival broke out. This caused great persecution in that village with the new converts being beaten and disowned. In sadness for the plight of these new believers, John pressed in further in prayer for God's intervention. After enduring this intense persecution by natives, Hyde began leading his fellow missionaries in intercession for India.

In 1896, there were no conversions at all, which greatly disturbed John Hyde. He locked himself away in prayer to "find the reason." In this time of intense intercession, the Spirit of God began to reveal that the "life of the church was far below Bible standards." So Hyde committed himself to leading by example through prayer, Bible study and declarations of faith. By 1899, he began spending entire nights facedown before God. In a letter to his college he wrote:

> Have felt led to pray for others this winter as never before. I never before knew what it was to work all day and then pray all night before God for another. . . . In college or at parties at home, I used to keep such hours for myself, or pleasure, and can I not do as much for God and souls?[10]

The more time he spent in prayer the less his fellow missionaries understood him. Some even thought him to be fanatical and extreme. But he was willing to be called crazy and face this religious opposition if his prayers somehow brought revival to India. Soon he was tagged with the nickname "Praying John Hyde," a moniker that has remained with him to this day.

In these times of intercession, God began giving Hyde a vision of what was to come for the Church. Between 1900 and 1901, he wrote home to tell others what the Lord had shown him in prayer.

> The new century would be a time of Pentecostal power, and a double portion of the Holy Spirit would be poured out. A great conviction would come and many would be born again. He saw full apostolic Christianity restored to the church. Hyde believed that a great revival would occur after an understanding of the baptism of the Holy Spirit. He often preached a message, "You Shall Receive Power After."[11]

Hyde was now completely sold out to prayer for the nation of India. So in 1904, he formed the Prayer Group Union for the purpose of "targeted intercession" for 30 minutes each day. The group prayed for revival, special blessings on the churches, and a spirit of unity, guidance and wisdom. That same year, Hyde and his fellow missionaries scheduled a gospel convention.

It was at this time that they heard of the revival that had begun in Wales, and this caused an increase in prayer and faith for the same. Thirty days before the meetings, they went into all-night prayer with fasting, crying out, pleading and agonizing over the lost. Hyde liked to pray prostrate on the floor. He would pray with people "til," as he described it. Such a spirit of intercession was on him that others too would begin to groan in agony for the lost. Over and over again, John Hyde's cry was, "Give me souls, O God, or I die!"

After he was done praying, he would clap his hands, dance and shout. He was often filled with holy laughter. The results of their prayers were plainly seen at the Sialkot Convention as a special anointing fell upon those gathered in 1904.[12]

"Year by year the prayer union fasted and prayed," says Richard Klein, "and at each convention a growing urgency for evangelism and intercession filled each attendee. John Hyde emerged as the prayer leader, and all were amazed at both the depth of his spiritual insight and the ferocity of his burden for India."

By 1908, John Hyde's faith had grown to the point where he dared to pray what was to many at the convention an impossible request: that during the coming year in India, one soul would be saved every day—365 people converted, baptized and publicly confessing Jesus as their Savior.

It seemed to be an impossible goal—yet it happened. Before the next convention John Hyde had prayed more than 400 people into God's kingdom. When the prayer union gathered again, he doubled his goal to two souls a day. Eight hundred conversions were recorded that year, and still Hyde showed an unquenchable passion for lost souls. Before the 1910 meeting ended, John Hyde revealed that he was again doubling his goal for the coming year— four souls a day, and nothing less.

During the next 12 months, John Hyde's ministry took him throughout India. The ministry of "Praying Hyde" was sought in

Calcutta, Bombay and other large cities across the nation. If on any day four people were not converted, Hyde said at night there would be such a weight on his heart that he could not eat or sleep until he had prayed through to victory.

The number of new converts continually grew. But John Hyde's health was rapidly deteriorating. Friends in Calcutta persuaded Hyde to see a doctor, as the years of travail had obviously taken a toll. No one expected the medical examiner's incredible diagnosis. John Hyde's heart had shifted out of its natural position on the left side of his chest to a place over on the right. It was unlike anything the doctor had seen before, and he warned Hyde that unless he got complete rest, he would be dead in six months.

But Praying John Hyde soldiered on, living for nearly two more years—long enough to see a wave of revival sweep through the Punjab and the rest of India. And he was able to live long enough to have his own personal vision enlarged. Before he died, he shared what God had shown him:

> On the day of prayer, God gave me a new experience. I seemed to be away above our conflict here in the Punjab and I saw God's great battle in all India, and then away out beyond in China, Japan, and Africa. I saw how we had been thinking in narrow circles of our own countries and in our own denominations, and how God was now rapidly joining force to force and line to line, and all was beginning to be one great struggle. That, to me, means the great triumph of Christ.[13]

In March 1911, John Hyde left India to seek medical attention in America. He arrived in Carthage, Illinois, to spend some time with his sister. Then on February 17, 1912, Praying John Hyde passed into eternity at the age of 47. His last words were "Shout the victory of Jesus Christ!"

The Welsh Revival
At the same time that God was working through John Hyde in India, He was moving powerfully in Great Britain. "Like a tree shaken by a

mighty storm, Wales was moved by the power of God until almost every home in the nation felt its impact," Kathie Walters says of the revival in the early twentieth century. "Newspapers in bold headlines carried the news of the amazing scenes taking place. So great was the fear of God, and conviction gripped the people, that in some communities crime disappeared. Magistrates were presented with a blank paper, no cases to be tried. To commemorate the occasion, they were presented with white gloves! In more than one place the post office's supply of money orders was exhausted as people sought to make restitution by paying their debts."[14]

It was reported that saloons and theaters were closed and stores were sold out of Bibles and New Testaments. Members of parliament, busy attending revival services, postponed their political meetings. Theatrical companies coming into districts found no audience, "for all the world was praying."

"This is revival," declared Rev. Owen Murphy, "when men in the streets are afraid to open their mouths and utter godless words lest the judgment of God should fall; when sinners, overawed by the presence of God, tremble in the street and cry for mercy; when, without special meetings and sensational advertising the Holy Ghost sweeps across cities and towns in supernatural power and holds men in the grip of terrifying conviction; when every shop becomes a pulpit; every heart an altar; every home a sanctuary and people walk softly before God—this is revival!"

"The Welsh Revival of 1904," continued Rev. Murphy, "was like a mighty tornado. The Spirit of God swept across the land until mountains and valleys, cities and villages were filled with the mighty manifestations of God. Churches were crowded and meetings went on day and night. Prayer, singing and testimonies would sweep over congregations in torrents, and hundreds turned to Christ. Never in the history of Wales had such indescribable scenes been witnessed."[15]

After experiencing this revival in Wales, Dr. G. Campbell Morgan returned to Westminster Chapel in London and declared, "Here is revival that comes from heaven; there is no preaching, no order, no hymn-books, no choirs, no organs, no collections and finally no advertising! Now think of that for a moment! There were organs—but they were silent. There were ministers—but there was no preaching—they were among the people praising God! Yet the Welsh revival is a revival of preaching, for everybody is preaching. No order and yet it moves from day to day, county to county with matchless precision, with the order of an attacking force. No song books, but—ah me, I nearly wept over the singing! When the Welsh sing they abandon themselves to the singing. No choir did I say? It was all choir."

"Wales is ablaze for God," he continued. "Already 50,000 converts have been recorded and the great awakening shows no signs of waning. It is sweeping over hundreds of villages and cities, emptying saloons, theaters and dance halls, and filling the churches night after night with praying multitudes. Go where you will; into the bank; the store; the trains. Everywhere men are talking about God."[16]

The Azusa Street Revival
Reporting on the Welsh Revival, writers for the *Yorkshire Post* told how young men and women who knew nothing of Old Welsh would speak that tongue under the influence of the Holy Spirit. On one occasion, a Dutch visiting pastor reportedly preached an entire sermon in English, even though he did not speak the language. This same phenomenon of "speaking in tongues" was appearing in America, spurred on by Rev. Charles Fox Parham of Bethel Bible School in Topeka, Kansas.

Like Praying John Hyde, Parham believed there was something more from God that the Church would need to meet the challenge of the new century. Dr. Vinson Synan gives this account of the events leading up to the outpouring of the Holy Spirit. "By December 1900, Parham had led his students thorough a study of the major tenets of the holiness movement. . . . When they arrived at the second chapter of Acts, they studied the events that transpired on the day of Pentecost in Jerusalem, including speaking in tongues. At this juncture, Parham had to leave the school for three days on a speaking engagement. Before leaving, he asked his students to study their Bibles in an effort to find the scriptural evidence for the reception of the baptism with the Holy Spirit.

"Upon returning, he asked the students to state the conclusion of their study, and to his 'astonishment' they answered unanimously that the evidence was 'speaking with other tongues.' This they deduced from the four recorded occasions in the Book of Acts when tongues accompanied the baptism with the Holy Spirit. Parham agreed with their conclusion and called a watch night service on December 31, 1900, which was to continue into the New Year. During the service, a student named Agnes Ozman asked Parham to lay hands on her head and pray for her to be baptized with the Holy Ghost with the evidence of speaking in tongues."[17]

Synan continues, "It was after midnight and the first day of the twentieth century when Miss Ozman reportedly began 'speaking in the Chinese language' while a 'halo seemed to surround her head and face.' Following this experience, Ozman was unable to speak in English for three days, and when she tried to communicate by writing, she invariably wrote in Chinese characters. This event is commonly regarded as the beginning of the modern Pentecostal movement in America. After Ozman experienced 'tongues' the rest of the students sought and received the same experience. Somewhat later Parham himself received the experience and began to preach it in all his services."[18]

It didn't take long for the news of what was happening to reach the press of Topeka and Kansas City. Reporters, government interpreters, and language experts soon rushed to the school to investigate the new phenomenon. A few days later, the *Topeka Capitol* reported in bold headlines: "A Queer Faith, Strange Acts . . . Believers Speak in Strange Languages." The *Kansas City World* reported, "These people have a faith almost incomprehensible at this day."

The wire services picked up the story when Parham and his students visited Galena, Kansas, in late January. The *Cincinnati Enquirer* reported that it was doubtful if anything in recent years had awakened the interest, excited the comment or "mystified the people" as the events in Galena.[19]

In 1901, Parham closed the school in Topeka and began a traveling revival ministry that lasted four years. In December 1905, he moved his headquarters to Houston, Texas, and opened another Bible school to teach his views on the baptism in the Holy Spirit. One of his students was an African-American man named William Seymour. With a deep desire for biblical training, Seymour enrolled in Parham's school, despite the system of racial segregation in the South at that time that forced him to sit in the hallway listening to the lectures through an open doorway. Seymour agreed with Parham's teaching that speaking in tongues was the sign of the baptism in the Holy Spirit, though he did not receive the experience at the time.

A woman named Neely Terry from Los Angeles, California, was visiting Houston and invited Seymour to visit her church with the possibility of becoming the pastor. The church was founded and led by Julia W. Hutchins and was a part of the Southern California Holiness Association. In his first sermon at the church, Seymour preached on Acts 2:4 and announced the necessity of speaking in other tongues as evidence of the infilling of the Holy Spirit. Pastor Hutchins was shocked by the radical teaching. She expelled Seymour from the church, and at the urging of the Holiness Association, locked the door, refusing to allow him to return.

Seymour was invited to stay in the home of Richard Asberry on Bonnie Brae Avenue where he started a series of prayer meetings seeking the baptism in the Holy Spirit. After several weeks of intense prayer, Seymour and the others gathered in the house received baptism with the gift of tongues on April 9, 1906. Soon there were so many people that they had to move the meetings out of the house where Seymour preached to the crowd, gathered in the street, from the front porch.

Soon they began looking for a facility to hold the revival services. They found an old building at 312 Azusa Street that had formerly been an African Methodist Episcopal church, but was now being used as a stable and warehouse. On April 14, 1906, Seymour led the first service on Azusa Street. Only four days later, the *Los Angeles Times* reported "a weird babble of tongues" in the midst of "wild scenes" in the mission. Within just a few weeks, more than a thousand people had gathered outside the 40-by-60-foot building to witness the outpouring of the Holy Spirit.

The Azusa Street Revival had begun.

By the end of 1906, Seymour officially incorporated his ministry as the Pacific Apostolic Faith Movement. He began publishing a magazine called *Apostolic Faith*, which soon had an audience of more than 50,000 subscribers—many who lived outside the United States. The news of the revival spread quickly and soon people from across the country and around the world traveled to Los Angeles to receive the baptism in the Holy Spirit. For three years the Azusa Street meetings continued, gathering three times a day, seven days a week. As a result the Pentecostal movement spread around the world—with related revivals reported in Jerusalem, India and China, and throughout Europe and South America.[20]

One of the most amazing aspects of the Azusa Street Revival was that every race and nationality mingled in the crowds that pressed into the mission in meeting after meeting. There was a total absence of discrimination as blacks, whites, Asians, Jews, and others sat side by side to hear the teaching of God's Word. Of the Azusa Street Revival, it was famously said, "The color line was washed away by the blood."[21]

The New Hebrides Awakening

The flames of revival eventually settled into a glowing ember throughout the first half of the twentieth century as the Church endured World War I, the Great Depression and then World War II. The great C. S. Lewis helped keep the embers of Christianity stoked when the British government invited him to give a series of radio broadcasts during the darkest days of the Battle of Britain—reminding the nation of its Christian heritage. Those broadcasts were eventually transcribed as Lewis's classic *Mere Christianity*.

But after six long years of war, and the Allies' victory over Nazi Germany, postwar Europe sought to return to normalcy. During this time, many Europeans abandoned the church as they tried to rebuild homes and families damaged or destroyed by war. On the

Hebrides Islands, off the coast of Scotland, not a single young person attended Sunday services after the war. "The islands, which had seen many revivals in the past, were now becoming a spiritual wasteland," says Scott Ross of *The 700 Club*.

But two elderly sisters of the islands refused to let the enemy have his way in their home. Peggy Smith was an 84-year-old blind prayer warrior. Her sister, Christine, suffered from severe arthritis. But despite their physical challenges, they prayed fervently for revival. God answered by giving Peggy a vision of Duncan Campbell, a famed Scottish evangelist, preaching on their island. She saw the churches filled with young people. So she called her pastor and declared, "I believe that Duncan Campbell ought to come." The minister was amazed. "My wife feels the same thing," he replied. "This must be of God." So at the mouth of two witnesses, the pastor invited Duncan Campbell to visit the islands.

But Duncan Campbell turned down the invitation, explaining that he was already engaged for another gathering of great importance.

Peggy and Christine were not swayed by Campbell's response, and they continued praying for revival. "They knew that Duncan Campbell would come just as God had shown them," Ross explains. The little lady exclaimed, "I won't accept that. He will come. God will make him come." She continued to pray as she encouraged the pastor. "Print the invitations and put them in all the roads."

Prior to receiving the invitation to go to New Hebrides, Campbell's granddaughter had asked him why God didn't work the same way as in the sermons that he preached. "This sent Duncan to his knees to offer God his willingness to go anywhere for revival," says Ross. "It wasn't long before God began to move."

According to Dr. Elmer Towns, Campbell was sitting on the front row of the Keswick Convention, which is the deeper life center of all of England. "He was the next speaker up when the Spirit of God came upon him and he felt conviction. He turned to the moderator and said, 'You will have to excuse me, God has another appointment for me.' He got up and walked away." Campbell got on a boat and made the journey to the Hebrides. He knew that

God was calling him there. It was in this little church that God broke through the hearts of people on these islands.

"He got off the boat at four o'clock in the afternoon," Dr. Towns explains. "Now there was a mailman waiting for him. And he said, 'We knew you would come. You have just enough time for high tea before the meeting.' He said, 'What meeting?' He answered, 'The announcements are all up. It starts tonight. Talk about God.'" He went to high tea, and then he went and preached.

The church was full. During the invitation a young man stood up and said, "I feel it up there—God is right up there and he wants to come down."

"Duncan went to the back door to shake hands as the parsons do," Towns explains. "He looked out the door and the yard was full of people. The Spirit of God had pulled them there and they came in. They stayed until four in the morning—and the Spirit of God came down. People began to get saved and to get right with God.

"Most of the bars were put out of existence. The churches were filled with young people. The church enrollment exploded. People came back to God. There was just tremendous healing of the land. Sin was being done away with. That revival went on for the next 30 years."

"God heard the fervent prayers of two housebound believers who were praying for revival," Scott Ross declares. "He transformed their island from a wasteland to a spiritual paradise. God still hears our prayers today. If we will draw near to Him, He will draw near to us."[22]

Through the Latter Rain and then the Charismatic movements, the power of the Holy Spirit continued to expand in the Church as the flame that was lit in the Azusa Street Revival was passed onward. The incredible outpouring of power through the Pentecostal and Charismatic movements has led many to call it the "Century of the Holy Spirit."

Now as we are well into not only a new century, but also a new millennium, God is calling for this generation to pick up the banner of revival and carry it forth, fanning the flames of renewal through prayer.

God wants to bring revival to you and to your part of the world—and He is looking for a people who will rise up and take hold of His promises in the Spirit realm, pulling them into the natural realm through prayer by faith. As you pray the news, led by the Holy Spirit, you are carrying the flames of revival to the next generation—preparing the world for the return of King Jesus!

LIVING ON A PRAYER

Pastor Anne Gimenez of Rock Church has often said, "As long as I have the Word of the Lord, I know that everything will be all right." This was her anchor in any storm. Having the Word of the Lord is the key to everything we receive from God—including our salvation.

God brings His Word to us in many ways. It may come through a friend sharing a Scripture verse, through a vanity plate driving down the highway, through a dream or vision, or simply seeing someone holding a John 3:16 banner at a football game. We may not even be looking for God. But God, in His mercy, comes looking for us! His Spirit begins to move upon us and He begins to reveal Himself to us. Then somewhere along the way, He brings His Word to us.

The psalmist declares, "Deep calls to deep at the sound of Your waterfalls" (Ps. 42:7). From the depths of His love and grace, the Spirit of the Lord begins to breathe upon the Word of the Lord that is planted in the depths of our spirit. Suddenly life springs forth where there was no life. Suddenly we begin to ponder the reality of God. Suddenly we are confronted with our sin. Suddenly we are confounded by the amazing sacrifice of Jesus on the cross. Suddenly the Scriptures are transformed from the *logos* of ancient written words on a page to the vibrant, living *rhema* (Holy Spirit utterance to you) of God.

The Word of God Is Alive

Ten years ago, I (Wendy) was given the privilege of co-anchoring Christian World News, a half-hour weekly program that focuses on global happenings in the Church and is seen around the world.

At the time, we always ended the show with a simple "Thanks for watching" and "Goodbye." I felt that something was missing. It seemed cold. I suggested that we say, "God bless you" at the end of each show. After all, it is "Christian World News." CWN Senior Producer Stan Jeter agreed.

Even when we're running short on time at the end of the show, I always try to squeeze in "God bless you"—even if I have to drop something else. I sometimes wondered if it really made a difference to anyone who was out there watching. In my spirit, I was fairly confident that it did, but I didn't have any proof, until recently.

A lady in Taiwan, we'll call her "Kim," was planning to commit suicide. She was going to end her suffering by jumping off the seventh floor of her apartment building. Although Kim was a Christian, she was deeply depressed because of some family issues. Fortunately, Christian World News, which airs in Taiwan on our sister station, Good TV, was on in the other room. At a very strategic moment, just as Kim was planning to head to the balcony and jump, she heard me say, "God bless you." She ran to the other room and shouted at the TV, "Come back, come back!" but the show was over and we were off the air. Still, that little bit of encouragement was enough to stop Kim from the unthinkable. She called a friend in the U.S. that she knew would have more words of comfort. She received prayer and healing.

She's now giving her testimony and is back on track with the Lord.

All I can say is, *Thank You, Lord. Thank You for saving Kim with those precious words, "God bless you."* And of course, it wasn't so much the words but the Spirit of God on those words. "It's not by might, nor by power but by my Spirit says the Lord Almighty" (Zech. 4:6). Now I look forward to saying those words on TV even more, knowing that somewhere in the world they may be saving a life.

By the miraculous grace of God, the seed of His Word planted in our hearts and watered by His Spirit springs forth into everlasting life like it did for Kim. Where once we were lost, we recognize that we have been found. Where once we were blind, we now see. The moment comes when we confess with our mouth that Jesus is

Lord, and believe in our heart that God raised Him from the dead—
and then we are saved (see Rom. 10:9-10)!

This same process is how we receive anything from heaven.
First, God reveals His Word and breathes on it by His Holy Spirit.
Then if we are open to His leading, our eyes become enlightened to
the gift that He wants to give us. We then take a step of faith and
corresponding action to receive the gift that He reveals through
His Word.

As Pastor Gimenez declares, if you have the Word of the Lord,
everything will be all right. To the born-again believer, the Word of
God is "the sword of the Spirit" (Eph. 6:17). We can use the Word
of God—the Bible, the Sword of the Spirit—both offensively and de-
fensively as we pray the news.

Adam and the Word of God

The apostle Paul gave us a clear contrast between what the Bible calls
the first Adam and the last Adam:

> So also it is written, "The first man, Adam, became a living
> soul." The last Adam became a life-giving spirit (1 Cor. 15:45).

The first Adam in Eden had the Word of the Lord not to eat from
the tree of the knowledge of good and evil. When the serpent came
to tempt them, Adam and Eve had the Word of God, the Sword of
the Spirit. They could have used it as a weapon against Satan. The
devil came at them with the three basic temptations that the apostle John speaks of in 1 John 2:16: the lust of the flesh, the lust of the
eyes, the pride of life (or possessions):

- The lust of the flesh: "The woman saw that the tree was
  good for food . . ."
- The lust of the eyes: "It was a *delight to the eyes* . . ." (v. 6,
  emphasis added)
- The pride of life: "The tree was desirable to *make one wise*"
  (Gen. 3:6, emphasis added)

Though they had the Word of the Lord, the Sword of the Spirit, they did not use it to deflect the lies of Satan, and they fell into temptation. As a result of this disobedience, the entire world fell into sin. Satan became the god of this world—the ruler of earth, holding the keys to death, hell and the grave.

Paul gives the contrast between the first and the last Adam in the book of Romans: "For as through the one man's disobedience the many were made sinners, even so through the obedience of the One the many will be made righteous" (Rom. 5:19).

We were made righteous through the obedience of the last Adam, Jesus Christ. He became our example of how to overcome Satan with the Word of the Lord. In the wilderness temptation recorded in Matthew 4, the devil used the same three basic attacks that he used against Adam and Eve:

- The lust of the flesh: "If You are the Son of God, command that these *stones become bread*" (Matt. 4:3, emphasis added)
- The lust of the eyes: "The devil took Him to a very high mountain and *showed Him all the kingdoms of the world and their glory*. . . . All these things I will give You, if You fall down and worship me" (vv. 8-9, emphasis added)
- The pride of life: "If You are the Son of God, throw Yourself down; for it is written, '*He will command His angels concerning You*'" (v. 6, emphasis added)

But Jesus refuted all of the enemy's temptations by using the Sword of the Spirit as His offensive weapon—deflecting every lie with the declaration, "It is written!"

In the first temptation, Jesus answered, "*It is written*, 'Man shall not live on bread alone, but on every word that proceeds out of the mouth of God'" (Matt. 4:4, emphasis added).

In the second temptation, Satan picks up Jesus' strategy and tries to twist the Word of God to use it in his deception. He declares, "If you are the Son of God, jump off! For the Scriptures say, 'He orders his angels to protect you'" (Matt. 4:6, *NLT*).

But Jesus is immediately aware of the devil's scheme and comes right back at him with the Sword: "The Scriptures *also say*, 'Do not test the Lord your God'" (Matt. 4:7, *NLT,* emphasis added).

In the third temptation, Satan shows his motive for the rebellion that he waged in heaven and that he still fights for the souls of men: "All these things I will give You, if You fall down and worship me" (Matt. 4:9).

Jesus has had enough at this point, and with one final thrust of the Sword, he declares: "*Go, Satan! For it is written,* 'You shall worship the Lord Your God, and serve Him only'" (Matt. 4:10, emphasis added).

The Gospel of Luke tells us that "when the devil had finished every temptation, he left Him until an opportune time" (Luke 4:13). In the original Greek of Matthew, the "devil left Him" is in the historic present tense, indicating a lack of permanence, meaning that the devil would later return to further tempt Jesus. But Satan could not prevail against the Lord because of the Sword of the Spirit—the Word of God.

As we pray the news, we need to follow the example of the last Adam, wielding the Sword of the Spirit and declaring, "It is written!" in answer to the devil's lies.

We often hear people say, "resist the devil and he will flee," which is good advice. But there is more to that passage through the apostle James that gives us the complete meaning:

> *Submit therefore to God.* Resist the devil and he will flee from you (Jas. 4:7, emphasis added).

We can't truly resist the enemy unless we first submit ourselves fully to God. This submitting to God is echoed in the passage from the book of Revelation that we spoke of earlier: "They did not love their life even when faced with death" (Rev. 12:11).

Jesus demonstrated this Scripture in how He overcame Satan, first in the wilderness with the word of His testimony, then at the cross by the shedding of His blood, loving not His own life even unto death. He took back from Satan the keys to death, hell and the grave.

So with the Word of the Lord, we can overcome in any and every circumstance. As we are praying the news, we will come up against the attacks and temptation of the enemy. We must resist his attacks in the same way Jesus did.

As you pray the news, God will give you assignments that will require great faith and persistence. You may receive a burden from the Lord in prayer that will take you to some very difficult places— both in the spirit and, possibly, in the natural. Despite all opposition from the devil and from people under his control, you must hold fast to the Word of the Lord. You must overcome every temptation, test and trial by the blood of the Lamb, by the Word of your testimony, loving not your life, even unto death—declaring, "It is written!"

Overcoming with the Word

The Word of the Lord can come to us in different ways—but it is always powerful when wielded against the enemy through faith-filled prayers and declaration. There may be times when the Lord will direct us to war in the spirit with a particular passage of Scripture. At other times, He may speak directly to our heart by His Spirit. Then there are those times when He will give us a prophetic word through another believer that is just for us to use as a weapon of warfare. Paul equips Timothy with this tool and reminds him to use it in spiritual battle:

> This command I entrust to you, Timothy, my son, in accordance with the prophecies previously made concerning you, that by them you fight the good fight (1 Tim. 1:18).

The word for "prophecies" in the Greek is the word προφητεία, *propheteia,* which means "prophetic utterance." This is the same word used by Paul in his letter to the Thessalonians when he declares:

> Do not quench the Spirit; do not despise prophetic utterances [προφητεία, *propheteia*] (1 Thess. 5:19-20).

Paul also uses this word in his discourse on the manifestation of the Spirit in his first letter to the Corinthians:

But prophecy [προφητεία, *propheteia*] is for a sign, not to unbelievers but to those who believe (1 Cor. 14:22).

In his instructions to Timothy, Paul is not telling him to wage war in the Spirit with the Scripture, but with the prophetic utterances that have been spoken over him by the manifestation of the Holy Spirit through other believers.

In addition to our use of Scripture in spiritual battle, we can also wage war with the prophetic words that have been spoken over us in prophetic ministry.

David and the Word of the Lord

Throughout the Bible, we see examples of men and women of God who received the Word of the Lord and then obediently moved out in faith—and as a result, received the promise given by God.

In 1 Samuel 30, we see where the Amalekites had come to the city of Ziklag, burned the city and captured the wives and children of David and his mighty men, taking them into captivity. When David and his men made this discovery, they were filled with grief. That grief turned to anger against David, and his men spoke of stoning him. But the Scripture says that David strengthened himself in the LORD (see 1 Sam. 30:6).

Then David called Abiathar the priest and asked him to bring the ephod so he could know the Word of the Lord. The Bible says:

David inquired of the LORD, saying, "Shall I pursue this band? Shall I overtake them?" And He said to him, "Pursue, for you will surely overtake them, and you will surely rescue all" (1 Sam. 30:8).

So David and his men were strengthened and encouraged by the Word of the Lord. In obedience they set out to take back their wives and their property. Scripture tells us the result of their obedience to the Lord's directive:

> So David recovered all that the Amalekites had taken, and rescued his two wives. But nothing of theirs was missing, whether small or great, sons or daughters, spoil or anything that they had taken for themselves; David brought it all back (1 Sam. 30:18-19).

The Disciples and the Word of the Lord

We see another example of this in the Gospel of Mark, during an exhausting season of ministry for Jesus and His disciples:

> On that day, when evening came, He said to them, "Let us go over to the other side." Leaving the crowd, they took Him along with them in the boat, just as He was; and other boats were with Him. And there arose a fierce gale of wind, and the waves were breaking over the boat so much that the boat was already filling up. Jesus Himself was in the stern, asleep on the cushion; and they woke Him and said to Him, "Teacher, do You not care that we are perishing?" And He got up and rebuked the wind and said to the sea, "Hush, be still." And the wind died down and it became perfectly calm. And He said to them, "Why are you afraid? Do you still have no faith?" They became very much afraid and said to one another, "Who then is this, that even the wind and the sea obey Him?" (Mark 4:35-41).

Jesus had given the disciples the Word of the Lord: "Let us go over to the other side." So despite the wind and the waves, they should have had peace that they would arrive safely at their destination. But the disciples were not yet mature, so when the storm rose up, instead of resting in faith, they were consumed with fear. But when the wind and the waves obeyed the command of Jesus, their faith took a quantum leap forward. After this Mark simply declares, "They came to the other side of the sea" (5:1).

Peter and the Word of the Lord

Luke gives us the account of Peter and the God-fearing Roman centurion, Cornelius. In a vision, during a time of prayer, Peter received a Word from the Lord that changed the course of the Church forever:

> While they were making preparations, he fell into a trance; and he saw the sky opened up, and an object like a great sheet coming down, lowered by four corners to the ground, and there were in it all kinds of four-footed animals and crawling creatures of the earth and birds of the air. A voice came to him, "Get up, Peter, kill and eat!" But Peter said, "By no means, Lord, for I have never eaten anything unholy and unclean." . . . This happened three times, and immediately the object was taken up into the sky. . . . While Peter was reflecting on the vision, the Spirit said to him, "Behold, three men are looking for you. But get up, go downstairs and accompany them without misgivings, for I have sent them Myself" (Acts 10:9-14,16,19-20).

Having received the Word of the Lord, Peter traveled with the men to the house of Cornelius where he entered and preached the gospel to all of the Gentiles gathered there. While he was still speaking, the Holy Spirit fell on Cornelius and his friends, and they all spoke in other tongues. Peter and the other Christian Jews rejoiced that the Holy Spirit had descended on the Gentiles as well.

Because of Peter's obedience to the Word of the Lord, in that moment, God's Word to Abraham that through him and his seed all the nations of the earth would be blessed was further established in the Early Church.

The Word and the Spirit

The Lord desires to lead us by His Holy Spirit as we pray the news. God is love, and love communicates. So God is communicating all of the time. The question is, are we listening to Him? He is always broadcasting—but are we tuned in to His frequency to know how we should pray? Once we have the Word of the Lord, then we move forward in obedience under the leading of the Holy Spirit. The Lord, speaking through Isaiah, declares to His people:

> Your ears will hear a word behind you, "This is the way, walk in it," whenever you turn to the right or to the left (Isa. 30:21).

In Brother Lawrence's classic writing *The Practice of the Presence of God,* this seventeenth-century French lay brother of the Carmelite Priorty speaks of the wonderful adventure of living a life that is led by the Spirit of God:

> The presence of God is the concentration of the soul's attention on God, remembering that He is always present.... The means of acquiring the presence of God ... is faithfully practicing God's presence. This must be done gently, humbly, and lovingly, without giving way to anxiety or problems. The soul's eyes must be kept on God, particularly when something is being done in the outside world.
>
> The first blessing that the soul receives from the practice of the presence of God is that its faith is livelier and more active everywhere in our lives. This is particularly true in difficult times, since it obtains the grace we need to deal with temptation and to conduct ourselves in the world. The soul—accustomed by this exercise to the practice of faith—can actually see and feel God by simply entering His presence. . . . Its faith becomes more and more penetrating as it advances through practice.[1]

Our sensitivity to the leading of the Spirit of God increases through purposeful seeking of Him in quiet times of prayer. We should find a special time every day that is set aside to be alone with God. This is a time for praise and thanksgiving, repentance, forgiveness, lifting up petitions and soaking in the presence of the Father. It is a time to be quiet before the Lord and journal the things that He speaks to us and the direction He gives us.

But life is not always convenient. We often juggle many different priorities and responsibilities. So we need to be sensitive to the leading of the Holy Spirit as we go through our daily routines, keeping our ears tuned to God's voice. We are promised in Romans 8:14 that those who are the children of God are led by the Spirit of God. As we pray the news, we can stand on this precious promise and believe that the Lord will guide us by His Spirit in intercession.

We have a co-worker at CBN, Jay Comiskey, who lives out this balance of daily routine with an ear tuned to the leading of the Holy Spirit. Though he has a very busy job at CBN, Jay is quick to respond to the direction of the Holy Spirit when he senses His leading.

On one particular winter day, Jay felt the leading of the Lord to go to Cape Henry in Virginia Beach to pray. Cape Henry is very strategic ground in the spirit realm, as it is the place where the English settlers planted a wooden cross they carried across the ocean and dedicated North America to the glory and purposes of God. Jay was crying out to the Lord, reminding Him that those English settlers had prayed that from these shores, the gospel would be carried to all the nations of the world. He prayed that through the ministry of CBN, the nations of the world would be reached for His glory. "God," he asked aloud, "what's on Your heart?" As soon as he uttered this prayer he turned and watched as a wave carried on to the shore an inflatable beach ball globe. He couldn't believe his eyes. Every nation of the earth was on this beach ball map of the world. Jay looked up and down the beach to see whose globe it might be, but he was the only person on the beach that day. He picked up the inflatable globe and carried it home with him.

It was clear what was on the Lord's heart: "God so loved the world . . ." (John 3:16)! Shortly after this happened, in an all-staff chapel at CBN, Jay told the story and then presented the globe to Pat Robertson with the declaration, "Pat, God has called CBN to go into all the nations and preach the gospel, and He sent this sign to remind us that this is our mandate." The CBN staff erupted in applause and praise.

In more than two decades, God has placed a tremendous burden on Jay's heart to pray for righteousness to be established on the United States Supreme Court. He has been involved in numerous prayer events and initiatives across America with well-known intercessors Dutch Sheets, Lou Engle and others praying that God's will be done on the High Court.

On one hot summer day in 2005, I (Craig) took my kids to visit the Smithsonian Institute in Washington, DC. After a long day of museum hopping, we were walking from Union Station over Capitol Hill to our subway stop. On our right was the Capitol Building, and on our left was the Supreme Court. While we were still some distance from the steps to the Court, I could see a familiar figure clad in shorts and a Hawaiian shirt, standing with a group of young people. It was Jay Comiskey! I turned and handed my camera to my son and said, "God's about to do something really cool. Take a bunch of pictures."

CRAIG AND JAY COMISKEY APPROACHING THE DOORS OF THE SUPREME COURT TO INTERCEDE JUST AFTER JUSTICE SANDRA DAY O'CONNOR ANNOUNCED HER RETIREMENT

Jay didn't see us coming as he was praying with the young people from The Call. I walked up behind him and said, "I think this may be a divine appointment." Jay turned in surprise and gave me a big hug.

"I think you're right, brother," he responded. "Do you want to go to the doors and pray?" We turned together and made our way up the wide granite stairs leading to the large bronze doors at the entrance to the Court. Sandra Day O'Connor had recently announced her retirement, and Chief Justice William Rehnquist was suffering with thyroid cancer. It was a pivotal moment in the history of the Supreme Court, and of our country as a whole.

My son took pictures as we placed our hands on the doors and prayed that God's perfect plan be done on the Supreme Court.

Within weeks, Justice William Rehnquist died and was succeeded by John Roberts as the Chief Justice of the Supreme Court. Only a few months later, Justice Samuel Alito was confirmed as Associate Justice. Both of these men are strong conservatives and pro-life, replacing the conservative Rehnquist and the moderate-to-conservative O'Connor.

These answers to prayer regarding the Supreme Court came after years of Christians like Jay praying the news for the High Court. As you respond to God's calling to intercession, He will give you various short-term assignments that will have a specific beginning, middle and end. But as you are faithful in your prayer ministry, He will also likely give you long-term intercessory assignments that will require years of prayer before the answers come. You may even receive a calling to pray for an issue or a need that you will not see an answer to in your lifetime. Praying the news is a never-ending spiritual battle.

This was the case with Jay and the Supreme Court. As he has prayed for the Court, God has introduced him to dozens of other prayer leaders with the same calling. One of those intercessors is Tom Hess, the coordinator of a ministry called Supreme Court Prayer Watch, whose goal is to see the 1973 *Roe v. Wade* decision overturned in America. Tom writes, "I believe we need to repent and ask God for forgiveness for our attitude which has tied God's hands from moving in this situation, ask the judges and others for forgiveness and loose forgiveness for them."[2]

In May 1986, God called Hess on a 40-day fast to believe Him to reverse the *Roe v. Wade* position. On the fortieth day of this fast, Chief Justice Warren Burger, who had been one of the authors of *Roe v. Wade*, said that *Roe v. Wade* should be re-examined, and then resigned as Chief Justice. William Rehnquist, a pro-life Associate Justice, was then appointed Chief Justice, and Antonin Scalia, an outspoken Christian, was appointed as an Associate Justice. In response to these monumental changes on the Supreme Court, Hess established a 24-hour prayer watch in August 1986.

Hess has seen other dramatic events occur after times of intense prayer and fasting. On Pentecost Sunday, June 7, 1987,

12 individuals affiliated with the Supreme Court Prayer Watch began a 21-day fast and solemn assembly for the abolition of abortion in America. On Friday, June 26, 20 days later, pro-abortion Justice Lewis F. Powell Jr., resigned from the Supreme Court.[3]

If God is calling you to pray the news, He most likely will call you to a lifetime commitment to a ministry of intercession like that of Jay Comiskey or Tom Hess. Be careful to consider the cost before you say yes to such a commitment. But if you do, the rewards for your obedience, both on earth and in eternity, will most likely be beyond your ability to comprehend.

Give Us This Mountain

In what is known as the Bible's faith hall of fame, the writer of Hebrews gives us examples of righteous people who stood firm in their belief that God would bring the answers to their prayers—just like Jay, Tom and other faithful intercessors are doing today. Some of them held on to the promises of God for years before they received from heaven. Some never saw the answer in their lifetime.

> All these died in faith, without receiving the promises,
> but having seen them and having welcomed them from
> a distance (Heb. 11:13).

At times, this calling to pray the news may require great persistence in the spirit. Caleb is an example to us of this kind of persistent faith. It was Caleb alone who joined Joshua in giving a positive report to the children of Israel about the Promised Land (see the story in Numbers 13:25–14:9). He knew that God had already promised the land to the Children of Israel. For Caleb it didn't matter that there were giants in the land—they would be driven out before the people of God!

Caleb and his family were promised an inheritance by God through Moses. He determined that he wasn't going to rest until he obtained the promise of the Lord. Forty years later, Caleb stood before Joshua, who had become the leader after Moses' death, and he boldly declared:

> You know what the LORD said to Moses the man of God at Kadesh Barnea about you and me. . . . On that day Moses swore to me, "The land on which your feet have walked will be your inheritance and that of your children forever, because you have followed the LORD my God wholeheartedly" (Josh. 14:6,9, *NIV*).

Then Caleb claimed his promise from the Lord:

> Now give me this mountain that the LORD promised me that day. You yourself heard then that the Anakites were there and their cities were large and fortified, but, the LORD helping me, I will drive them out just as he said (Josh. 14:12, *NIV*).

As we pray the news in obedience to God's leading, we will have our mountains to take for the Kingdom. Though there may be spiritual forces that we confront, by faith we can drive them out because we have the promise of God that He has given us the land. Because Caleb wholeheartedly followed the Lord, the God of Israel, the Bible tells us that:

> Joshua blessed Caleb son of Jephunneh and gave him Hebron as his inheritance. So Hebron has belonged to Caleb son of Jephunneh ever since (Josh. 14:13-14, *NIV*).

There is a mountain to take in the spirit realm. We do that by persistent obedience to the ministry of intercession by the leading of the Holy Spirit. The Lord has called the Church to be an end-time watchman on the wall. This is His word through Habakkuk:

> I will stand on my guard post and station myself on the rampart; and I will keep watch to see what He will speak to

me, and how I may reply when I am reproved. Then the LORD answered me and said, "Record the vision and inscribe it on tablets, that the one who reads it may run" (Hab. 2:1-2).

An important part of the ministry of reconciliation (see 2 Cor. 5) that God has given to the Church in this hour is to cast vision and equip the people of God that they may run with that vision to fulfill the call of God on their lives. We need to diligently seek God in prayer for this vision and for the wisdom and boldness needed to make the truth plain to our brothers and sisters in Christ so that they may be thoroughly equipped.

The prophet Habakkuk spoke of the power of vision from God:

For the vision is yet for the appointed time; it hastens toward the goal and it will not fail; though it tarries, wait for it; for it will certainly come, it will not delay (Hab. 2:3).

Let us be persistent in our pursuit of the Lord, pressing in for His vision so that we can be like the sons of Issachar (see 1 Chron. 12:32), advising spiritual Israel on what needed to be done.

"Do you think the news business represents an important institution in our culture?" asks Joseph Farah of WorldNetDaily. "Are you upset about the way it sometimes distorts events and portrays the kingdom of God in negative ways? Have you done anything other than to complain about it?

"I believe there is only one thing holding back a major spiritual revival in our country today: a lack of fervent prayer and fasting for that revival."

The great Bible teacher E. M. Bounds wrote concerning this pressing need for people of prayer:

The crying need of the times is for men, in increased numbers—God-fearing men, praying men, Holy Ghost men, men who can endure hardness, who will count not their lives dear unto themselves, but count all things but dross for the excellency of the knowledge of Jesus Christ, the Saviour. The men who are so greatly needed in this age of the Church are those who have learned the business of praying.[4]

Will you answer God's call to pray the news and become this kind of intercessor?

Praying for Ourselves

In a conversation with Jim DeSantis, a former local news director for a CBS affiliate, I asked how he would advise people to pray the news. He answered, "If you take it down to the personal level, maybe the prayer ought to be for ourselves and our discernment—to apply the principles of the Bible to what we're hearing and seeing."

So how do you pray for yourself as you process the information you are taking in from the news media? "Everything starts at home," DeSantis explains. "It's like the kid who says, 'I want to change the world.' Well before you can change the world, you have to change your country; and before you can change your country, you have to change your state; and before you can change your state, you have to change your city; and before you change your city, you have to change your neighborhood; and before you change your neighborhood, you have to change yourself."

"I talk to God," Jim says, "and I do it in Jesus' name, because He's my doorway. My heart feels that anguish—and to me, that's a prayer. Prayer, to me, is having a relationship with God through the Holy Spirit, in Jesus' name. When my spirit is feeling anguish or sadness about an event, that to me is prayer.

"There's tremendous power in prayer. Prayer moves mountains. When you get enough people praying, you can move mountains."

Praying the news requires a heart of service and humility to guard against praying for our own desires instead of the Lord's will. There can be a fine line between interceding earnestly for a particular thing and praying for our own desires to be fulfilled.

Instead, we need to seek to be humble servants of both God and our fellow man through our calling as intercessors. This ministry of intercession is truly a high calling that must be approached with wisdom and humility. As we follow the direction of the Master in intercession, we must seek to be wise as serpents and harmless as doves (see Matt. 10:16).

We must be like John the Baptist, who understood the preeminence of Christ as he declared, "He must increase, but I must decrease" (John 3:30). If we want to see true change occur, we must yield fully to the direction of the Holy Spirit in our prayers. There will be times when we won't know what to pray and we must allow the Holy Spirit to pray through us.

> In the same way the Spirit also helps our weakness; for we do not know how to pray as we should, but the Spirit Himself intercedes for us with groanings too deep for words (Rom. 8:26).

There is no limit to what God can do through a believer who is totally surrendered to His will. Mother Teresa, who was recognized with the Nobel Peace Prize and honored by heads of state, religious leaders and journalists around the world, said of herself, "I am a little pencil in the hand of a writing God who is sending a love letter to the world." This is the heart attitude that God can use to truly shine His light in the darkness.

Now Go Forth and Pray the News!

The prophet Isaiah declared:

> A voice is calling, "Clear the way for the LORD in the wilderness; make smooth in the desert a highway for our God. Let every valley be lifted up, and every mountain and hill be made low; and let the rough ground become a plain, and the rugged terrain a broad valley; then the glory of the LORD will be revealed, and all flesh will see it together; for the mouth of the LORD has spoken" (Isa. 40:3-6).

We know that John the Baptist fulfilled this prophecy in part when Jesus was born. But Bible-believing Christians are now a part of the end time that Elijah prophesied would be preparing the way for the return of the King. As we co-labor with him in praying the news, we are helping to raise up the valleys, preparing the way for the government to be on the shoulders of the Messiah. And when that day comes when Jesus returns, we will rejoice to see . . .

> The tabernacle of God is among men, and He will dwell among them, and they shall be His people, and God Himself will be among them, and He will wipe away every tear from their eyes; and there will no longer be any death; there will no longer be any mourning, or crying, or pain (Rev. 21:3-4).

As you accept this calling to pray the news, go forth with confidence that God will be with you and will guide you by His Holy Spirit. Attempt great things for God! Expect great things from God!

10

GO AND DO

As I (Craig) was growing up, my father often instructed me, "Do the thing that you know God has called you to do, and do it with all of your heart, and soon you will be known as the person who does that thing."

Everyone should pray the news, but some will have a burden and a calling to do so as a ministry. Do you know that you have that calling to pray the news? Then begin today.

Prayer to Direct Your Steps

To start your journey of intercession, take a moment right now to consecrate yourself to this holy calling. Find a quiet place alone with God—it could be at your home, in your prayer closet, bedroom, office, porch or patio. Some people like to go outdoors to be with the Lord—a hike in the forest or a long walk on the beach. Wherever it is, come into His presence with thanksgiving and praise. Thank Him for the blessing and privilege to be called into this wonderful ministry. Then ask Him to fill you with His Holy Spirit and direct your steps.

Ask the Lord to give you His anointing for the work that He has called you to do, for "the yoke will be destroyed because of the anointing" (Isa. 10:27, NKJV).

You may want to speak with your pastor and ask him to assemble the elders and key leaders of your church to pray over you and anoint you with oil. If they move in the gifts of the Spirit, the Lord may use them to minister prophetically over you during this time. You may want to have a digital recorder on hand to record this session. You can then transcribe the prophetic words that are spoken and use them for encouragement and guidance at a later time.

Partners to Keep You Accountable

Ask the Lord to give you a prayer partner and an accountability partner. This may be the same person, or it could be two different individuals. These people can be local or you can communicate with them online through Facebook, Skype or email. A prayer partner can pray with you or pray individually but communicate with you and encourage you from time to time. An accountability partner is someone who helps you stay on task. This is someone who can check in with you occasionally—maybe every week or once every other week—to make sure you are keeping your commitment to pray the news. You can call upon either one of these people for prayer support and encouragement if you are feeling discouraged or weary in your ministry.

Every ministry is built on prayer. Find people who will commit to praying for you as you pray the news. Send them an update every couple of months to share the fruit of the ministry and remind them to pray. We can't do it alone. The Body of Christ needs every member doing his/her part in order for the whole Body to be effective in representing Jesus in the earth today.

A Prayer Journal to Keep You Tuned In

If you don't have a prayer journal, buy one. It doesn't have to be elaborate, unless you want it to be. A spiral-bound notebook will work just fine. Or you may be someone who does everything digitally. Whatever works for you is fine. Just make sure you have something on hand to write down the things the Lord shows you to pray about.

Begin by observation. When I (Craig) was in journalism school at Regent University, our professors taught us to learn how to pay closer attention to what was happening in the world around us. "Learn how to be curious," one teacher instructed. "Carry a notebook everywhere you go," another exhorted, "and write down the things you observe. Little things can sometimes turn into big stories."

It's the same with the ministry of intercession, though the prayer warrior must learn to be sensitive to what is happening in both the natural and the spiritual realm.

As we stated earlier, ask the Lord to lead you to sources of news that will give you a balanced view of events from both sides of the political spectrum. Don't limit yourself to just one outlet for your news. Look at a mix of sources—television, newspaper, online, magazines, radio, e-newsletters, and so on. Here are some examples of the leading sources for news that you may want to consider, both secular and Christian (in alphabetical order, with no rank of importance or significance):

- ABC News
- Assist News Service
- Bloomberg News
- BBC News
- CNN
- CBN News
- CBS News
- *Charisma* magazine/news
- *Christianity Today* magazine
- The Drudge Report
- The *Economist*
- *Forbes* magazine
- Fox News
- The Huffington Post
- The *Jerusalem Post*
- The *London Times*
- The *Los Angeles Times*
- MSNBC
- NBC News
- The *New York Times*
- *Newsweek* magazine
- PBS
- Reuters
- *Time* magazine
- *US News and World Report*
- *USA Today*
- The *Wall Street Journal*

- The *Washington Post*
- The *Washington Times*
- The *Weekly Standard*
- WorldNetDaily.com

As you watch, read or listen to the news, the Holy Spirit will highlight a particular story that He will want you to pray for. If you are able, lift up a prayer at that very moment.

God will often put a burden on your heart for a story or a person in the news and will remind you to pray again and again. Yield to the Holy Spirit and intercede for these things until the Lord lifts the burden from you, or the headlines change.

When Waiting for Answers to Prayer

You've read some amazing stories in this book about people who prayed the news and saw incredible breakthrough. But there will also be many times when we will not see the results of our prayers in this lifetime. Do not be discouraged if you don't see a dramatic breakthrough in the headlines regarding a story that God has placed on your heart. Just continue to pray whenever the Lord reminds you. The apostle Paul said, "Be joyful always, pray continually, give thanks in all circumstances; for this is God's will for you in Christ Jesus" (1 Thess. 5:16-18, *NIV*).

Charles Spurgeon, the famous nineteenth-century English preacher, noted that "'pray continually' comes right after 're-joice always,' as if that command had somewhat staggered the reader and made him ask, 'How can I always rejoice?' and, therefore, the apostle appended an answer, 'Always pray.' The more praying, the more rejoicing. Prayer gives a channel to the pent-up sorrows of the soul, they flow away, and in their stead streams of sacred delight pour into the heart. At the same time, the more rejoicing the more praying; when the heart is in a quiet condition and full of joy in the Lord, then also will it be sure to draw nigh unto the Lord in worship. Holy joy and prayer act and re-act upon each other."[1]

As we have already shared, you may receive a burden to pray for something in the news and then you will possibly intercede for that for the rest of your life.

William Wilberforce was a godly man and a member of the British Parliament who had a tremendous burden to see the slave trade ended. He prayed and worked his whole life for this cause and only saw the slavery abolished just weeks before his death.

We often quote from the first half of chapter 11 of the book of Hebrews, what is known as "the faith hall of fame." But we often forget about the courageous men and women of God mentioned in the second half of that chapter who stood boldly in faith, yet did not see the answer to their prayers in their own lifetimes:

> All these died in faith, without receiving the promises. . . .
> And all these, having gained approval through their faith,
> did not receive what was promised, because God had pro-
> vided something better for us, so that apart from us they
> would not be made perfect (Heb. 11:13,39-40).

It is in their example of patience, courage and trust in God that these saints have received the answer from God to their prayers despite the fact that they didn't see the answer during their life on earth. Allow these brave men and women of God to encourage you when you get discouraged over what may seem to be unanswered prayers.

Jesus said it best: "Have faith in God" (Mark 11:22). And it is vital that we are led by the Holy Spirit in our prayers. Jesus taught His disciples: "But when He, the Spirit of truth, comes, He will guide you into all the truth" (John 16:13).

The Holy Spirit is a person. We can pray and ask the Holy Spirit to direct us in our prayers. Ask Him to show you what to pray for and how to pray. Learn to be sensitive to the leading of the Holy Spirit. And when you sense the Spirit directing you to pray, stop right then, if you are able, and pray as He directs.

There may be an urgent situation requiring agreement in prayer that God will bring to your attention. It is important to pray when you sense this kind of urgent prompting of the Holy Spirit. We may never know until we get to heaven how our prayers made a difference in the lives of people as a result of our obedience to the Holy Spirit.

Most importantly, keep your relationship with God your top priority. Loving God with all your heart comes first. Then your ministry to your neighbor comes out of the overflow of that intimate relationship with the Father, Son and Holy Spirit. Jesus said:

> If you abide in Me, and My words abide in you, ask whatever you wish, and it will be done for you. My Father is glorified by this, that you bear much fruit (John 15:7-8).

The fruit of our ministry comes forth as a result of our first abiding in Jesus.

So go forth and pray the news as the Holy Spirit leads. You are God's ambassador and minister of reconciliation in the earth (see 2 Cor. 5). You are His hands and feet and mouthpiece, declaring, "Your kingdom come. Your will be done, on earth as it is in heaven" (Matt. 6:10). By faith, take the authority that God has given you, and through prayer and petition, with thanksgiving, stand in the gap as an intercessor praying the news.

God isn't interested in numbers. Throughout Bible history, the Lord often used only a remnant of people to get the job done. But He is looking for a few dedicated souls who will pray the news. We believe that if you've picked up and read this book, that person is you. One person really can make a difference.

And always remember . . . your prayers are more powerful than you know!

ENDNOTES

Preface
1. Delores Liesner, www.deloresliesner.com. © 2011. Used with permission.
2. Anne Arvizu, © 2011. Used with permission.

Chapter 1: We've Got to Pray Just to Make It Today
1. Ted Baehr, www.movieguide.org. © 2011. Used with permission.
2. Judson Cornwall, *Incense and Insurrection* (Shippensburg, PA: Destiny Image Publishing, 1986), pp. 47-48.
3. Lou Engle, cited in Derek Prince, *Shaping History Through Prayer and Fasting* (New Kensington, PA: Whitaker House, 2002), pp. 7-9.
4. Ibid.
5. H. G. Wells, *Mind at the End of Its Tether,* cited in Leonard Ravenhill, "Weeping Between the Porch and the Altar," © 1994 Leonard Ravenhill, Lindale, Texas. http://www.ravenhill.org/weeping1.htm.
6. Dennis M. Howard, "The Abortion Index," Movement for a Better America, © 2011. http://www.movementforabetteramerica.org/abortionindex.html.
7. Prince, *Shaping History Through Prayer and Fasting,* pp. 7-9.
8. C. S. Lewis, *Letters to Malcolm: Chiefly on Prayer,* quoted in *The C. S. Lewis Bible, New Revised Standard Version* (New York: HarperOne Publishers, 2011), p. 1159.
9. Ibid.
10. Ibid.

Chapter 2: Knowing Your Authority in Prayer
1. Rees Howells, quoted in Peter Lundell, *Prayer Power: 30 Days to a Stronger Connection with God* (Grand Rapids, MI: Revell, 2009), pp. 200-201.
2. Ibid.
3. Norman Grubb, *Rees Howells: Intercessor* (Fort Washington, PA: Christian Literature Crusade, 1959), cited William R. Wilkie, "Life in the Melchizekek Order VIII: Rees Howells and the Second World War," May 13, 2011. http://080808onnowto.blogspot.com/2011/05/life-in-order-of-melchizedek-viii-rees.html.
4. Lundell, *Prayer Power: 30 Days to a Stronger Connection with God,* pp. 200-201.
5. Dutch Sheets, *The Beginner's Guide to Intercessory Prayer* (Ventura, CA: Regal, 2001), p. 45.
6. A. R. Fausset, *Fausset's Bible Dictionary* (Grand Rapids, MI: Zondervan, 1949), "reconciliation." http://www.studylight.org/dic/fbd/view.cgi?word=reconciliation&search.x=0&search.y=0&search=Lookup&action=Lookup.
7. Ibid.
8. Ibid.
9. Ibid, "kingdom of heaven." http://www.studylight.org/dic/fbd/view.cgi?number=T2191.

Chapter 3: Understanding the News
1. Nancy B. Kennedy, © 2011. Used with permission.
2. Thomas Carlyle, *On Heroes, Hero Worship and the Heroic in History* (London: James Fraser, 1908), p. 392. http://www.online-literature.com/thomas-carlyle/heroes-and-hero-worship/.
3. Brian S. Brooks, George Kennedy, Daryl R. Moen and Don Ranly, *News Reporting and Writing,* fifth ed. (New York: St. Martin's Press, 1996), p. 11.
4. Ibid., p. 13.
5. Michael Schudson, *Discovering the News* (New York: Basic Books, 1981). http://history ofjournalism.onmason.com/2009/12/03/review-of-chapter-4-from-discovering-the-news/.

6. Bernard Goldberg, *Bias: A CBS Insider Exposes How the Media Distort the News* (New York: Regnery Publishing, 2001).

7. John Milton, *Areopagitica.* http://books.google.com/books/about/Areopagitica.html?id =w_4QAAAAIAAJ.

8. Thomas Jefferson, inaugural address, *The Papers of Thomas Jefferson,* vol. 33, 17 February to 30 April 1801 (Princeton, NJ: Princeton University Press, 2006), pp. 143-148. http://www.princeton.edu/~tjpapers/inaugural/inrevdraft.html.

9. Bonnie St. John, *How Strong Women Pray* (Boston, MA: FaithWords, 2007), pp. 216-218.

Chapter 4: How to Pray the News

1. Derek Prince, *Shaping History Through Prayer and Fasting* (New Kensington, PA: Whitaker House, 2002), pp. 71-75.

2. Ibid.

3. Ibid.

4. E. M. Bounds, *The Necessity of Prayer* (Radford, VA: Wilder Publications, LLC, 2008). http://www.revivallibrary.org/catalogues/miscellanies/prayer/boundsness.html.

5. Candy Arrington, © 2011. Used with permission.

6. Peter Lundell, *Prayer Power: 30 Days to a Stronger Connection with God* (Grand Rapids, MI: Revell Publishing, 2009), p. 102.

7. Ibid.

8. Ibid., pp. 102-104.

9. Ibid.

10. Bonnie St. John, *How Strong Women Pray* (Boston, MA: FaithWords, 2007), pp. 34-36.

11. Isaac Penington, quoted in Richard Foster and James Bryan Smith, *Devotional Classics,* "Letters on Spiritual Virtues" (New York: HarperOne, 2005). http://home.comcast.net/~pastorbob/devotional/isaacpennington.htm.

Chapter 5: The City of Hope

1. Becky Spencer, © 2011. Used with permission.

2. Julie Gillies, © 2011. First published in "A Battle for Peace" in *Proverbs 31 Woman* magazine. Used with permission.

Chapter 6: Prayer for Believers in the News Business

1. "The State of the News Media: Key Findings," Pew Project for Excellence in Journalism, 2010. http://stateofthemedia.org/2010/overview-3/key-findings/.

2. Deb Wuethrich, © 2011. Used with permission.

3. Chris Mitchell, © 2011. Used with permission.

4. Joseph Farah, © 2011. Used with permission.

5. Mark Martin, © 2011. Used with permission.

Chapter 7: Praying the Headlines

1. "Hostage: Here We Are Living Like the Living Dead," *The Greenville News,* Greenville, SC, December 2, 2007.

2. Marcia Moston, © 2011. http://marciamoston.blogspot.com Used with permission.

3. Dutch Sheets, quoted in "Dutch Sheets: Praying for Our Nation," *The 700 Club.* http://www.cbn.com/700club/features/dutch_sheets.aspx.

4. Janet Teitsort, © 2011. Used with permission. http://www.facebook.com/JanetTeitsort.

5. Lynetta Jordan, © 2011. Used with permission.

6. Sara Ann Friedman, "Alternate Report to the Initial Report of the United States of America to the U.N. Committee on the Rights of the Child Concerning the Optional Protocol to the Convention on Rights of the Child on the Sale of Children, Child Prostitution and Child Pornography," U.N. Committee on the Rights of the Child, 2007, p. 14. ecpatusa.org/wp-content/uploads/.../Alternative-Report-USA-Final-2007.pdf.

7. Donna Collins Tinsley, © 2011. Used with permission.

8. Jeanne Gowen Dennis, © 2011. Used with permission.
9. Janet Teitsort, © 2011. Used with permission. http://www.facebook.com/JanetTeitsort.

Chapter 8: Praying the News to Revival

1. Bonnie St. John, *How Strong Women Pray* (Boston, MA: FaithWords, 2007), pp. 122-123.
2. Julie Arduini, © 2011. Used with permission.
3. Martin Luther, quoted in Richard Foster and James Bryan Smith, "Excerpts from 'Table Talk,' 'Epistle Sermon, Fourth Sunday in Advent,' and 'Treatise on Good Works,'" *Devotional Classics* (New York: HarperOne, 2005). http://www.epm.org/resources/2011/Jan/28/great-quotes-prayer/.
4. Press release written for Williams College, October 2006. http://www.markrondeau.com/haystacklegacy.html.
5. "Haystack Prayer Meeting," Wikipedia.org. http://en.wikipedia.org/wiki/Haystack_Prayer_Meeting#References.
6. Press release written for Williams College, October 2006. http://www.markrondeau.com/haystacklegacy.html.
7. Scott Ross, "Layman's Prayer Revival," *The 700 Club*. http://www.cbn.com/spirituallife/churchandministry/churchhistory/FOR_LaymansPrayer.aspx.
8. "John Nelson Hyde," Wikipedia.org. http://en.wikipedia.org/wiki/John_Nelson_Hyde.
9. Richard Klein, "Profiles in Prayer: Praying John Hyde," *The 700 Club*. http://www.cbn.com/spirituallife/PrayerAndCounseling/Intercession/praying_john_hyde.aspx.
10. Ibid.
11. "John Hyde," Higher Praise Ministry. http://www.higherpraise.com/preachers/hyde.htm.
12. Ibid.
13. Richard Klein, "Profiles in Prayer: Praying John Hyde."
14. Kathie Walters, *The Bright and Shining Revival*. http://www.identitynetwork.net/apps/articles/default.asp?articleid=73082&columnid=2093.
15. Vinson Synan, *The Holiness-Pentecostal Tradition* (Grand Rapids, MI: Wm. B. Eerdmans Publishing Co, 1971), pp. 89-92.
16. Stanley M. Burgess, Gary B. McGee and Patrick H. Alexander, *Dictionary of Pentecostal and Charismatic Movements* (Grand Rapids, MI: Zondervan, 1988), pp. 780-781.
17. Synan, *The Holiness-Pentecostal Tradition*, p. 99.
18. Ibid.
19. Ibid.
20. Ibid.
21. Ibid.
22. Scott Ross, "Flames of Revival: New Hebrides Awakening," *The 700 Club*. http://www.cbn.com/spirituallife/BibleStudyAndTheology/Discipleship/Flames_of_Revival_New_Hebrides_Awakening.aspx.

Chapter 9: Living on a Prayer

1. Brother Lawrence, *The Practice of the Presence of God* (New Kensington, PA: Whitaker House Publishers, 1982), pp. 67-71.
2. Tom Hess, Supreme Court Prayer Watch brochure, undated.
3. Ibid.
4. E. M. Bounds, "The Weapon of Prayer: The Necessity for Praying Men," *CBN.com*. http://www.cbn.com/spirituallife/prayerandcounseling/intercession/weapon_prayer_0303c.aspx.

Chapter 10: Go and Do

1. Charles Spurgeon, Sermon number 1039, delivered on March 10, 1872, Metropolitan Tabernacle, Newington, England. http://www.spurgeon.org/sermons/1039.htm.

RECOMMENDED RESOURCES

Books

Baier, M. B., ed. *The C. S. Lewis Bible, New Revised Standard Version.* New York: HarperOne Publishers, 2011.

Brother Lawrence. *The Practice of the Presence of God.* New Kensington, PA: Whitaker House Publishers, 1982.

Burgess, Stanley M., Gary B. McGee and Patrick H Alexander. *Dictionary of Pentecostal and Charismatic Movements.* Grand Rapids, MI: Zondervan, 1988.

Cornwall, Judson. *Incense and Insurrection.* Shippensburg, PA: Destiny Image Publishing, 1986.

Foster, Richard J. *Prayer: Finding the Heart's True Home.* New York: HarperOne, 1992.

Frenn, Jason. *The Seven Prayers God Always Answers.* New York: FaithWords, 2011.

Grubb, Norman. *Rees Howells: Intercessor.* Philadelphia, PA: CLC Publishers, 1988.

Jeremiah, Dr. David. *Prayer: The Great Adventure.* Colorado Springs, CO: Multnomah Publishers, 2004.

Johnson, Bill. *When Heaven Invades Earth.* Shippensburg, PA: Destiny Image Publishers, 2005.

Lundell, Peter. *Prayer Power: 30 Days to a Stronger Connection with God.* Grand Rapids, MI: Revell Publishing, 2009.

Meyers, Glenn. *Seeking Spiritual Intimacy.* Downers Grove, IL: Intervarsity Press, 2011.

Prince, Derek. *Shaping History Through Prayer and Fasting.* New Kensington, PA: Whitaker House, 2002.

Robertson, Pat. W. *The Secret Kingdom.* Nashville, TN: Publishing Group, 1994.

Sheets, Dutch. *The Beginner's Guide to Intercessory Prayer.* Ventura, CA: Regal, 2001.

———. *Intercessory Prayer.* Ventura, CA: Regal, 1996.

St. John, Bonnie. *How Strong Women Pray.* Boston, MA: FaithWords, 2007.

Synan, Vinson. *The Holiness-Pentecostal Tradition.* Grand Rapids, MI: Wm. B. Eerdmans Publishing Co., 1971.

Wilkinson, Bruce. *The Prayer of Jabez.* Colorado Springs, CO: Multnomah Publishers, 2000.

Online Articles

Bounds, E. M. "The Necessity of Prayer." http://www.revivallibrary.org/catalogues/miscellanies/prayer/boundsness.html.

Websites

Prayer and Spiritual Resources

24-7 Prayer: www.24-7prayer.com

John and Carol Arnott, Catch the Fire: www.catchthefire.com

TheCall: www.thecall.com

CBN: www.cbn.com

CBN prayer resources: http://www.cbn.com/spirituallife/prayer andcounseling/intercession/)

Christian International (Bill, Tom and Jane Hamon): www.christianinternational.com

The Elijah List: www.Elijahlist.com

Eternal Perspectives Ministries (great quotes on prayer): http://www.epm.org/resources/2011/Jan/28/great-quotes-prayer/

Generals International (Cindy Jacobs): www.generals.org

Higher Praise Ministry: www.higherpraise.com

Identity Network: www.identitynetwork.net

International House of Prayer (IHOP): www.ihop.org

Iris Ministries (Roland and Heidi Baker): www.irismin.org

Dr. David Jeremiah: www.DavidJeremiah.org

National Day of Prayer: nationaldayofprayer.org

Charles Spurgeon's sermons: http://www.spurgeon.org/sermons/1039.htm.

Stormie Omartian: www.stormieomartian.com
Dr. Cindy Trimm: www.trimminternational.com

News and Opinion Outlets
ABC news: www.abcnews.go.com
Assist News Service: www.assistnews.net
The Blaze: www.theblaze.com
Bloomberg News: www.bloomberg.com
BBC News: www.bbc.co.uk
CBN news: www.CBNNews.com
CBS news: http://www.cbsnews.com
Charisma Magazine: www.charismamag.com
Christianity Today: www.christianitytoday.com
CNN: www.cnn.com
The Drudge Report: www.Drudgereport.com
The Economist: www.economist.com
Forbes Magazine: www.forbes.com
FOX News: www.Foxnews.com
The Huffington Post: www.huffingtonpost.com
The Jerusalem Post: www.jpost.com
The Los Angeles Times: www.latimes.com
MSNBC: www.msnbc.msn.com
The New York Times: www.nytimes.com
Newsweek magazine: www.newsweek.com
PBS: www.pbs.org
Reuters: www.reuters.com
Time magazine: www.time.com
The Times of London: www.thetimes.co.uk
US News and World Report: www.usnews.com
USA Today: www.usatoday.com
The Wall Street Journal: www.wsj.com
The Washington Post: www.washingtonpost.com
The Washington Times: www.washingtontimes.com
The Weekly Standard: www.weeklystandard.com
WorldNetDaily.com: www.wnd.com

AUTHOR CONTACT INFORMATION

Wendy Griffith
Wendy.Griffith@cbn.org

Craig von Buseck
www.vonbuseck.com
http://facebook.com/craigvonbuseck
http://blogs.cbn.com/ChurchWatch/
http://twitter.com/craigvonbuseck
http://www.cbn.com/about/bios/craigvonbuseck.aspx

To purchase the DVD *Appalachian Dawn* (the story of
God's transformation in Manchester, Kentucky), visit

www.communitychurch.net

or call

(606) 598-8871

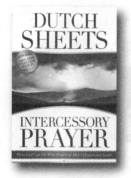